OUR EXCLUSIVE SOCIETY

OUR EXCLUSIVE SOCIETY

BY RACHEL RODNEY

NEW DEGREE PRESS

OUR EXCLUSIVE SOCIETY

ISBN

978-1-64137-972-4   *Paperback*

978-1-64137-851-2   *Kindle Ebook*

978-1-64137-852-9   *Digital Ebook*

To my family,
whose constant love and unwavering support
inspires me to pursue my dreams.

And to the makers,
who are building an inclusive society
for everyone to achieve theirs.

CONTENTS

———

AUTHOR'S NOTE

Many experiences inspired me to write this book. I started seeing how compounded disparities affected access to resources in my own community after studying abroad in South Africa, where other students questioned the nature of human rights in a way I had never been exposed to before. HuskyADAPT, a club at my university that started out as something I joined for fun—soldering circuitry to make accessible toys—was a mental break from calculus and chemistry. This club led me to pursue another opportunity where I researched the experience of people using upper limb prosthetics with Dr. Jennifer Mankoff, co-director of CREATE at the University of Washington, and Dr. Saiph Savage, co-director of the Civic Innovation Lab at Universidad Nacional Autonoma de Mexico. With them I learned about how much community affects factors that will make experiences work—or not.

I wouldn't have sought out any of these experiences if I hadn't discovered the way my mom's leg brace had deteriorated part of her body. When I touched the place where the brace supported itself on her leg, it was skin against bone. No body. The device that has enabled my mom to walk all of my life—from cooking, going to grocery stores, being the owner of an ice cream store, and later, a cafe—was hurting her. I was angry. Why hadn't a better solution been designed? Don't physical therapists and doctors and engineers know this can't be healthy?

My parents' hard work gave me the privilege of pursuing an education in engineering and I was eager to learn more about designing prosthetics. I jumped at every opportunity I could get to learn more about accessible design, which is what eventually lead me to inclusive design. My research for this book showed me there is not enough. There is not enough action being taken toward inclusivity, because for our society to become inclusive, it is going to take a change in both mindset and practice.

We won't achieve this by waiting for new guidelines to be implemented. We will achieve this by expanding who we envision the people using our products to be, learning about them, and including them in the design process.

My hope is in reading this book, you will start to question the "who" and "why" of things— and if the experiences are exclusive, think about what you can do to make an impact. And do it.

INTRODUCTION

"Everyone has the right to freely participate in the cultural life of a community, to enjoy the arts, and to share in scientific advancements and its benefits."

—UNIVERSAL DECLARATION OF HUMAN RIGHTS[1]

---

1   "The Universal Declaration of Human Rights," Universal Declaration of Human Rights, United Nations.

What comes to mind when you hear the word "exclusive?"

The exclusion this book talks about is the kind that bars people from participating in experiences we take for granted every day. This experience can be understanding a pop culture reference, entering a building, or feeling comfortable in the clothes we choose to wear.

A community that pops into mind when thinking about exclusion are people with disabilities. We're starting to better understand the challenges they face, which is why laws making things more accessible, like the Americans with Disabilities Act, have been put in place. Big names such as Beyoncé, Nike, and Domino's Pizza have had lawsuits filed against them for not being ADA compliant in their services.

Here's a statistic: The World Health Organization (WHO) says 15 percent of the world's population has some form of disability. This is over one billion people.[2] Additionally, the WHO says "rates of disability are increasing due to population aging and increases in chronic health conditions, among other causes." Many of us already have a disability—seen or unseen—and if we don't, we may develop one as we age.

Here's another statistic: By 2044, the populations we consider as minorities are going to become the majority in the US. [3]

These two statistics show that the people of our world are diverse in many ways, whether it be physical ability or cultural

---

2   "Disability and health," Newsroom, World Health Organization.

3   "Inclusion and Employee Diversity: Here are the Numbers," Analytics in HR.

roots. With this much diversity, why aren't we already inclusive? It could be because of our individualistic nature, which leads us to design for ourselves. Or it could be because we just don't know how.

People who make anything for other people need to approach their work with an inclusive mindset. This can include building infrastructure, designing physical or digital products, planning opportunities, or developing tools. At each step—from coming up with the idea to testing it—inclusion should be a consideration; however, inclusion isn't going to be part of any process unless people (a) know about it, and (b) care.

Misconceptions about inclusive creation make people unwilling to pursue it; however, companies have a lot to gain by being more inclusive—starting with having an inclusive mind. A way to do this is by having an inclusive workplace. This naturally feeds into creating more inclusively through each person influencing others and sharing their different views and experiences. Some statistics from Teamable show just how much a company can benefit with more inclusion in its workplace:[4]

- 2.3 times more money

- 1.7 times more likely to be leaders of innovation in that industry

- 70 percent more likely to grow into new markets

---

4   "6 Statistics That Will Convince You to Prioritize Diversity & Inclusion," Teamable Blog, Teamable.

Personally, I'm not driven by these statistics. What motivates me to do my part in creating a more inclusive society is the hundreds of stories of exclusion affecting us every day.

SO...WHY SHOULD WE CARE?

Nelson Mandela said "freedom cannot be achieved unless the women have been emancipated from all forms of oppression." I believe this is the same case for all marginalized communities. We, as a society, will be captives to harmful stereotypes and assumptions that lead to destructive action if we do not become more inclusive. In light of the events of 2020, the coronavirus pandemic has exposed how quickly people can become susceptible to xenophobia, and how crucial (and possible) digital accessibility is. The abhorrent injustices highlighted by the murders of George Floyd, Ahmaud Arbery, and Breonna Taylor and the painful country-wide response is the only way people feel like they can be heard. The black community is done with being discriminated against. They are done being seen as lesser, and our exclusive society is what enables this prejudice. We must stop, because it is devastating our communities.

Did you know in China, Muslims are being put into "re-education" camps? It's been happening for years, but what is anybody doing about it? In India, rural communities are being taken advantage of by powerful people, and young children are forced to go into dangerous mines for mica—the powder that makes our makeup sparkle. Why isn't their government involved? And here, in the US, why don't we hear about the police brutality against the LGBTQ+ community, especially against people of color?

When I first started writing this book, I thought I wanted to focus on accessible design. However, the more I learned about the communities being excluded in society, the more I discovered this book is really about the people making our society more inclusive.

I was compelled to write this book about inclusion because exclusion is something I have felt growing up. One thing a Korean girl said to me once pretty much sums it up:

"Wow, you're biracial? I really want my kids to be biracial too, so that they can be part of two cultures!"

This was an interesting concept, but sometimes it's like being part of neither. There was always something off about the way I felt with either primarily Korean kids or primarily white kids. This was in the back of my head as I started at the University of Washington (UW) in the State Academic RedShirt (STARS) program to improve diversity in UW's engineering departments. Over the first couple years, I heard about people's hardships and how much they had to fight for themselves to get to where they were. By the time I entered the department of Human Centered Design and Engineering, I began seeing and thinking about how other factors of a person's life could also lead to exclusive experiences. As I saw the exclusion, I started also seeing the efforts being made to foster inclusion; however, I didn't have the resources to actually learn about all of these things from my classes. Knowing something exists and knowing how to do it ourselves are two very different things. To learn more, I sought out people in the community who were making an impact by "inclusifying" experiences affected by exclusion.

WHAT DOES THIS BOOK TALK ABOUT?

Topics I write about under the lens of inclusive design are:

- **Accessibility.** People's differing abilities are not always considered when creating.

- **Diversity.** Diverse backgrounds and cultures are not often represented in varying spaces.

- **Equity.** People's economic status can impact their education and resources.

- **Education.** Makers in all industries lack essential knowledge about how to be inclusive and how to design inclusively.

- **Sexism.** The rights people have are not put into action based on gender.

- **Ageism.** The trend towards "new" and "young" are devaluing the experience levels of people...based off how much more experience they have?

These topics don't encompass everybody—this is just a starting point, stories applicable to what we are doing to get us thinking about even more communities.

A lot of conversation surrounding inclusion has been occurring and a lot of work has been put into making things inclusive, like American Eagle Outfitters' inclusive body campaign and the diverse cast of *Hamilton*. Some companies, like Adobe and Microsoft, have entire inclusive design departments. But these have not been widely adopted. Instead, what we see are buzzwords like "empathy" and "assumption" being thrown around with no real value underlying their use.

I believe inclusion should be considered in all designs, whether they be services or physical products. To address the problem effectively, we need to learn how to incorporate inclusion into teaching curriculums and practice. In this book, I will explore inclusion from different angles—with implications from the tech industry to applications in everyday life.

These insights about inclusive design are for emerging designers or researchers like me. Don't design only for those you think will be the largest consumers of your product (which are probably modeled subconsciously on your own abilities and culture). This is where assumptions and biases come in.

Throughout the chapters in this book, I might use some words differently than how they are typically understood. Here are some quick definitions:

- **Design.** I talk about design in the broadest sense of the word: deciding how something will work or look. This includes designing services and communities on top of designing technology and graphics. On social media I've seen people say, "We don't need another design sprint to solve our problems." I agree, in the sense that design sprints don't necessarily bring about immediate tangible change. However, we can apply design to create things that result in effective and immediate change.

- **Maker.** Anyone who is part of the creation process! This includes the people who came up with the idea, all the way to the people implementing it. They are making some part of the design process happen—and they don't have to be designers or builders to be considered a maker.

In this book, we will get glimpses into the world of geopolitics from Kate Edwards, CEO of Geogrify; Microsoft's design process of emojis in the area of race and alternate cultural norms from Danielle Oberst Salisbury; and we'll see how Allie Thu, a designer, is implementing change in her organization to increase inclusion and accessibility in the services provided.

While reading this book, understand there are communities I haven't been able to write about, but you might be able to support. My goal wasn't only to show you these communities, but to get you thinking about other people you might affect or relate to in some way, along with a few ideas on how to make society more inclusive for everyone.

PART 1

INTRODUCTION TO INCLUSIVE DESIGN

This section is a short introduction to inclusive design. Here we will explore different definitions related to the inclusive design space, and the history of inclusive design. We will also look at why it is important to design inclusively and how exclusion can affect people.

THE TL;DR HISTORY OF INCLUSIVE DESIGN

"In order to design inclusively, designers need to consider the widest range of possible users and environments."

—JIM THATCHER[5]

---

5   Jim Thatcher et al., *Constructing Accessible Web Sites* (Apress, 2002).

Every year I was in high school, I loved participating in National History Day. I would start doing research in the summer and spend a lot of time thinking about and prototyping my exhibits. National History Day is a competition where students research a history topic that has to do with that year's theme and create something to present it. This creation could range from a website, to a skit, to an exhibit. After spending the majority of four years researching history and learning about different people like Harry Hopkins (an important figure in WWII), or different events like the capture of the USS Pueblo (a US ship that is still held "captive" in North Korea—don't worry, most of the crew came back alive), I thought researching the history of inclusive design would be a similar feat. However, when I started looking, there wasn't a straightforward storyline. Instead, my understanding of inclusive design evolved from different sectors and came together as the framework it is now.

For this book, I am mainly going to talk about the broader scope of inclusive design, with accessible design and universal design as subsets. Imagine inclusive design is the umbrella with accessible and universal design under it. Accessible and universal design both flow into inclusive design. Steven Lambert from *Smashing Magazine* once stated, "The more inclusive you are to the needs of your users, the more accessible your design is."[6]

---

6   Steven Lambert, "Designing for Accessibility and Inclusion," *Smashing Magazine*, April 9, 2018.

TIMELINE

Here's a short timeline I gathered from the Institute of Human Centered Design:[7]

1950: Began barrier-free design by removing obstacles in the built environment

1970: Moved away from specialized adaptions for people and "toward the idea of normalization and integration"

Mid-1970s: Began forming the disability rights movement inspired by the Civil Rights Act

1990: The Americans with Disabilities Act was passed

Each one of these events resulted from the hard work of individuals coming together as one, showing how powerful change from the bottom up can be. The timeline mostly boils down to three types of design: universal design, inclusive design, and accessible design. I have heard these terms be used interchangeably at times—mostly universal design and inclusive design.

DEFINITIONS

I can't remember when I first heard of inclusive design. I thought universal design was what inclusive design was, but when I brought this up to my professor, he told me universal design is more related to built environments and inclusive design was what I was trying to pursue. When I mentioned this to other people I interviewed, one person thought the

---

7   "History," Inclusive Design, Institute for Human Centered Design.

same as I did at first, and another was like, "No, universal design is ONLY for buildings." With these mixed understandings, here are some definitions to clear up how I will address the different types of design.

ACCESSIBLE DESIGN

"A primary focus of accessibility is access by people with disabilities. The larger scope of accessibility includes benefits to people without disabilities." [5]

Accessible design was first seriously considered in the US after WWII, when many wounded veterans were now in need of accessibility facilitators, such as wheelchair ramps. This started the conversation and contributed to the creation of the ADA.

UNIVERSAL DESIGN

"The design of products and environments to be usable by all people, to the greatest extent possible, without the need for adaptation or specialized design." [8]

When I first began writing this book, I used the term "universal design" a lot because I wasn't sure what the difference between universal design and inclusive design was. In this book, I want to touch on all types of user experiences—not only physical products and built environments, but also the inclusion of different identities and cultures. However, the principles of universal design are still important to utilize and design for.

---

8   Bettye Rose Connell et al., "The Principles of Universal Design," April 1, 1997.

INCLUSIVE DESIGN

"In order to design inclusively, designers need to consider the widest range of possible users and environments." [5]

Inclusion means enabling everyone to participate in an experience. To design inclusively, the thing being designed needs to be able to allow anyone to participate and utilize it. Realistically there will always be constraints, but with the mindset of being inclusive, more people can use the product, and it may potentially become a better design for other users as well.

The users on the outskirts are typically thought of as small minorities—however, this is changing very quickly. Populations of people who are considered the minority are becoming the majority, and the longer people live, the more prone they are to developing ability barriers in the current physical environment.

"Inclusive design more accurately communicates our conviction that this practice is a continuous process of evolving ever more responsive solutions to a changing human reality. We witness different patterns of functional limitations, rising rates of natural disasters, and increasing socio-economic disparities. There may not be a single solution that works for all but a quest for balance of everyone's needs matters." [6]

With our constantly evolving world comes constantly evolving needs, and by considering all of them, we can create a more inclusive world.

Before people began recognizing the need for inclusion, acts against humanity were rooted in the exclusive nature of our societies. For example, before WWII in the US, people in prisons and homes for those with cognitive disabilities underwent forced sterilization. You would think that after WWII, this form of eugenics would have ended; however, according to *Indy Week*, it increased into the 1970s, continuing and expanding horrifically.[9]

"On a June morning in Alabama, a mother was told that her twelve- and fourteen-year-old daughters needed 'shots.' There were Latina women in Los Angeles and New York who couldn't even read the so-called consent forms. Gay men and lesbians. Cheyenne, Navajo, and Sioux women in the West, black women in North Carolina, and in Georgia, poor whites. In New York City, a mother asked doctors to sterilize her sixteen-year-old daughter just because the girl was going to attend a mixed-race camp that summer." [9]

These people underwent forced sterilization because of the exclusive social mindset that it was not okay to be different, so they should not be allowed to participate in contributing to the future of society.

Our exclusive society naturally elevates the needs of some people over the needs of others. Typically, the groups we cater to are the people in power since they are making the decisions. In working to change this system, inclusive design can be a strength, because in the process of designing inclusively, we have to learn about other cultures and different ways of life. Our greatest success can be achieved when we incorporate a diverse set of users and designers in the process.

---

9   Kevin Begos, "The American eugenics movement after World War II," *INDY Week*, May 18, 2011.

I HAD NO ONE TO HUG

—

"If we cannot now end our differences, at least we can help make the world safe for diversity."

—JOHN F. KENNEDY

The first time I remember being exposed to how certain populations were maltreated was in elementary school, when we went to Chinatown for a field trip. One of the stops was a museum about the Japanese internment camps the United States made to remove Japanese people from society out of fear they were spies during WWII. The pictures on the walls of the museum were of classrooms, with several empty desks where the students' Japanese-American classmates used to sit. One day they were there, and the next, they were shipped off to an internment camp. I wondered if that's how German students had felt when their Jewish counterparts stopped showing up to school.

At the time, I felt immensely sad for the students that no longer sat at their desks—they were the same age I had been at that moment. I felt scared and betrayed that the country I lived in would do that—creating a xenophobic "us versus them" mentality. Now that I'm older, I feel angry because of the many other stories of exclusion the United States hid from our education growing up.

They didn't teach me about eugenics.

They didn't teach me that Native Americans were given pox-infested blankets.

They didn't teach me that brutality against black Americans didn't end with Jim Crow laws.

History isn't just stories of what happened before we were born—they illustrate what is possible to resurface in our future. I honestly didn't know racism still existed in our society until I was in high school. In class, we talked about slavery, the Civil War, and Jim Crow laws, but everything was in the past. Except when we look at the news or when we talk to people, it isn't in the past. It's now.

I once went to a small play in Capitol Hill, a district in Seattle known as an LGBTQ+-friendly neighborhood. It was about three black lesbian women who become victims of police brutality—and nobody hears about their deaths. They never end up in the news. After the play, I learned there were so many people in the audience that had witnessed the same thing happen in their social circles, and how when their friends had been killed, nobody cared.

What else don't I know?

While I was studying abroad in India, my friend and I were sitting in the back of a rickshaw talking about exclusion. She was telling me about how, for the last few years, Muslims were being locked up in internment camps.

There's an article in *BBC News* about how "leaked documents detail for the first time China's systematic brainwashing of hundreds of thousands of Muslims in a network of high-security prison camps." Although China claims these camps are voluntary, the way these "voluntary" inmates are treated says otherwise.[10]

This isn't a small population being forced into "re-education." "About a million people—mostly from the Muslim Uighur

---

10   "Data leak reveals how China 'brainwashes' Uighurs in prison camps," *BBC*, November 24, 2019.

community—are thought to have been detained without trial."[10] These people were being forced into re-education internment camps for the sole crime of having different beliefs.

The scope of societal exclusion is, in itself, diverse. World-wide, exclusion occurs quite frequently, and the same thing is happening in local communities and within families and friend groups.

DISCRIMINATION AND HEALTH

The discrimination that is physically harming groups of people is bad—but why care SO MUCH about the social discrimination our peers experience all the time? Beside the fact it isn't fair, and discrimination and exclusion violate human rights, being discriminated against causes negative physical health consequences as well.

An NPR reporter compiled stories from people researching this space of discrimination and health. One of the researchers they interviewed said even though the occasional stress from being discriminated against may not have a significant immediate effect, being stressed in this way over time may create more noticeable effects.[11]

"Prolonged elevation [and] circulation of the stress hormones in our bodies can be very toxic and compromise our body's ability to regulate key biological systems like our cardiovascular system, our inflammatory system, [and] our

---

11   Rae Ellen Bichell, "Scientists Start to Tease Out the Subtler Ways Racism Hurts Health," *NPR*, November 11, 2017.

neuroendocrine system," [Amani] Nuru-Jeter says. "It just gets us really out of whack and leaves us susceptible to a bunch of poor health outcomes."[11]

Due to the situational and long-term effects of discrimination, the findings from this type of research are not often conclusive.[11] However, they do expose that discrimination inflicts deeper wounds than what we can see.

THE ISSUE OF FORCED DIVERSITY

When I posted on Facebook about how I was writing a book about inclusion, my friend Aaron from high school reached out to me about how he might have some perspective of trying to create inclusion for others, while facing exclusion. The conversation I had with him in a public library in our hometown showed me how much he had changed over the last four years with his experiences in college and knowing, in the field he is going into as a career, he is going to be a minority of a minority. The first being he is a man going into teaching, and the second being a *Latino* man going into teaching. He is not only going to face forms of exclusion in his gender, but also his race. In the United States, during 2015-16, 77 percent of public school teachers were female, and 23 percent were male. At this same time, only 9 percent of public school teachers were Hispanic.[12]

As an RA (resident advisor), Aaron has needed to teach his residents basic life skills, such as doing laundry and cooking ramen, all while creating a safe community.

---

12   "Characteristics of Public School Teachers," National Center for Education Statistics, Institute of Educational Science.

In creating and sustaining this community, he learned about reconciling differences in diversity. Since some people had not been exposed to the LGBTQ+ community before college, they invited someone from the Pride Center to talk about it. Another time they promoted diversity was during an exercise where the multicultural coach sat in the lobby and asked students to write down their name and what it means so they could put it up on the wall. One of the students got upset about this activity and started arguing about forced diversity. As a person of color, my friend was saddened by this incident and about how opposed this student was to celebrating diversity.

I know forced diversity is something people get upset about, and when thinking about why, I believe maybe it is because whatever diversity meeting or activity they are participating in is NOT about them. It is about someone else, a someone else who has probably lived their entire life experiencing the exact opposite, where everything has to be about and in accordance with the majority's traditional way of life. Now, whenever the majority is not the "intended audience" of the experience, they get upset about forced diversity.

When it comes to "forced diversity," everyone is entitled to their own opinions...but are their opinions based on the fear of not being the most important voice in the room, or are they based on facts? When people get upset about diversity, they aren't thinking about the opposite perspectives. I really liked this Twitter thread from a gamer:

"As a straight white dude my whole life has been filled with cool white dudes in gaming and comics...There's literally a million different choices you could pick from and think 'oh I want to be like them, I can relate to them.'"

"And now we're seeing more women, more people of color, more people of varying sexual orientations, and dudes are asking, 'Why does my character have to be gay?', 'I like this character but why do I have to play as a black girl?'"

And to be honest, y'all been playing as the 'straight white dude' for so long you're treating that as the default setting in life."[13]

This view of diversity in gaming can be applied everywhere else people get upset about diversity. By not accepting and incorporating diversity, people can be hurt and affected in ways they shouldn't based on their differences. Even at a diversity retreat, my friend felt excluded.

"All the people who identified as a person of color in the retreat, they just kind of like grouped in together just so they could voice their thoughts without, like, white people there, because it's really a different environment," Aaron explained. "And I noticed I was the only male Latino. There were a bunch of female Latinas. There were male and female African-Americans. And so, at the end everyone got really emotional, everyone's hugging each other...and I realized I didn't have anyone to hug."

---

13   Li Nefas, "Gamers Are Getting Upset over 'Forced Diversity', but This 'Straight White Dude' Shuts Them Down in a Viral Twitter Thread," *Bored Panda*, 2019.

It hurt my heart to hear my friend say this. In all the years I've known him, I've never seen him as anyone other than a super supportive and positive person who would always be there for anyone. Listening to Aaron's story of how he felt excluded even though he was surrounded by a community celebrating diversity was painful. I wish I could have taken away these emotions and told myself he wasn't going to face this again in his life, but that isn't possible. Aaron knows how much exclusion hurts and is making it his goal to support and be there for children in situations similar to his own. Aaron is going into teaching as a career where he is a minority on two different fronts. Knowing this, he takes the instances of exclusion he has experienced and transforms them into learning experiences so he can better prepare himself to face what is coming up in his life.

With his typical optimistic view on life, Aaron told me, "I can't say it's going to be graceful, but I can say it's not going to be disastrous."

HIRING QUOTAS

Another problem with having this form of exclusion in the workplace is the stigma around hiring quotas, something he's seen happen between his peers in college—before they even enter into the careers for which they are getting degrees! The toxic mindset of whether or not someone was hired to fill a quota or because they had the genuine skills required for the job is beginning to infect people before they join the workforce.

"There's a 'friend' that I have—and I put 'friend' in air quotes—who applied for a job, and he didn't get it...for reasons I do know and totally agree with. But he was complaining to some other people that, like, the reason he didn't get it is because he was white, he was straight, and cis. And so, like, those are the reasons he didn't get hired, and they were just filling the quota… and he was saying this to my trans friend that got hired…when he said that he was basically just saying, 'My qualifications are irrelevant. And they only got hired based upon things they can't control, rather than, like, what they were qualified to do.'"

Aaron's "friend's" mindset diminished the validity of the acceptance that his other friend received after getting the job, even though he didn't get hired for specific reasons. But Aaron couldn't tell him that, so now this "friend" is living with the mindset that someone got the job solely because they are a minority.

After witnessing this toxic mindset degrade the importance of diversity in so many other instances, Aaron admits he feels like he is becoming numb to the exclusion.

"When you live in a college campus and you're exposed to a lot of different viewpoints, you will experience a lot of ones that you disagree with….I've gotten numb to it, and it sucks."

This feeling is shared among many other people and it's growing at a dangerous rate. It puts people into the mindset that maybe things will never get better. It is crucial to start implementing inclusion now—talking about it is not enough, and it is burning people out. Even when I looked up "forced diversity" on Google, I found a forum with people complaining about having to go to diversity meetings every year. This burnout and unwillingness to learn shows that people aren't seeing things change in the community fast enough. However, what they may not realize is that they are what is needed to make inclusion become a reality.

Being against cultural diversity makes people in minority groups think they will never be truly accepted, to the point of causing negative effects on mental health. These negative feelings surrounding diversity should be eradicated to save both the person in the minority group and the person in the majority group from feeling upset, which is counterintuitive to creating a safe world for everyone. Both the presence and absence of inclusion changes people.

Exclusion led Aaron to become stronger as he will continue to be a minority throughout his career, but he still feels the emptiness and the sense he is lacking community. Exclusion led Aaron's friend to feel unsafe in their identity at their workplace. How many more people share these types of experiences? I think everyone has on different levels, but maybe they don't recognize it because it is the societal norm, or maybe they do recognize it and don't do anything about it because it is also an established norm. Being inclusive in mindset would eliminate these misconceptions about forced diversity and hiring quotas, because then people would be valued based off what they do instead of how they look.

LET'S INCLUSIFY

- Practice being aware of how your actions are discriminatory, purposefully or not; discrimination causes negative health affects over time.

- Practice identifying the many ways in which people can be excluded from different angles.

PART 2

INCLUSIVE MAKERS

This section is a compilation of stories about what I learned from makers who are creating inclusive experiences both locally in the United States and abroad. Their stories cover a range of different marginalized communities for whom we can design. Please keep in mind these chapters do not include all the possible communities we might not be considering, but rather some of them. It is my aim that in reading about creating inclusively for these communities, you might consider the needs of other communities.

While you are reading, don't hesitate to whip out your preferred note-taking device and jot down your thoughts!

SEXISM...IT'S
EVERYWHERE

---

*"Other women who are killing it should motivate you, thrill
you, challenge you, and inspire you."*

—TAYLOR SWIFT

Once I began college, I was able to start recognizing things I had been warned about earlier. I noticed people repeating something I said after I had said it just a few minutes before, and the dwindling number of women in my STEM classes, like programming. During my study abroad term in India, I started a conversation with someone who was beginning his own startup. He was well-known in his community for his hacking abilities, and he used these skills to create a virus to infect programs that detected viruses. One day, a group of us got together and he told us about how he had spent the day learning how to use machine shop tools. When I engaged in conversation with him about this, remembering my own high school days in a machine shop making electric cars, he did not seem happy that I even knew what he was talking about.

However, in the Human Centered Design and Engineering department, I didn't feel that way. I didn't feel like there was a large rift between men and women in STEM, or that I was any form of minority in tech. Later, I realized it was because about half of the students in the program are women—not a statistic shared in the other engineering departments. My comfort in HCDE was due to the gender diversity of the program, which led me to understand the importance of being part of diverse communities. I have learned that one strategy which contributes to having more gender diversity is including more women in leadership roles.

In "Bold & Untold" by the MAKERS YouTube channel, I learned about Millie Dresselhaus, the woman who helped developed the field of nanotechnology through innovative research in physics. She won two presidential medals: the Presidential Medal of Freedom (from President Barack Obama in 2014) and the National Medal of Science (from President George H.W. Bush in 1990).[14]

Dresselhaus was only one of two female professors at MIT in 1960, and at that time, only 4 percent of the student body were women. In a COMSOL blog post by Bridget Cunningham, I learned:

"Dresselhaus often found that she was quite isolated in her science classes. In fact, she was many times the only woman in her class. That caused her to ask the question: Why aren't we women doing more?"

"I've always believed that women could lead," Dresselhaus said. "You have to learn how to create opportunities for yourself so you can do what you want to do."[15]

Some other women who have worked hard to create opportunities for themselves who I didn't know about until doing research for this book are:[16]

- Ginni Rometty, CEO of IBM

- Indra Nooyi, CEO of PepsiCo

- Marissa Mayer, CEO of Yahoo

---

14 MAKERS, "She Invented the Tiny Tech That Allows You to Watch Videos on Your Phone," October 30, 2018, video, 1:30.

15 Bridget Cunningham, "Mildred Dresselhaus, a Driving Force for Women in STEM," *COMSOL Blog*, March 7, 2016.

16 Laurence Bradford, "15 of the Most Powerful Women in Tech," *The Balance Careers*, June 25, 2019.

- Safra Catz, CEO of Oracle

- Sheryl Sandberg, COO of Facebook

- Susan Wojcicki, CEO of YouTube

These companies are huge, and people know them around the world; yet, I never realized the leaders of these prominent companies were women.

There are other women who are leaders and have become essential mentors in my college career. They have made an impact on me and who I will think about as women who have carved a path for me so I can continue carving paths for others. One of them is Dr. Lauren Bricker, an assistant teaching professor in computer science at the University of Washington (UW). I was honored to be able to interview her for this book and learned so much more about women in tech and how to use the experiences of exclusion to garner empathy for others to create a more inclusive world.

AN EXPERIENCE OF BEING A WOMAN IN TECH

"I kind of kept my head in the sand a lot about being one of the few women in the room when I was going through college and grad school and then working because it was, I think in a way, kind of painful to notice." explained Dr. Bricker.

Looking up my professor's LinkedIn profile before interviewing her for this project was a weird experience. In the last two years, I had viewed Dr. Bricker first as the magenta-haired professor who passes out rubber ducks we can talk to while debugging code. After attending her office hours throughout the year, she became a mentor I knew I could rely on for advice and motivation. Her dedication to teaching and coming up with new ways to present concepts made me warm up to her. During this time, all I really knew about her background was after some industry experience, she became a high school computer science teacher, then later taught computer science at UW. After this interview I learned that the high school where she taught is where Bill Gates and Paul Allen went, and she had a lot of industry experience before going into teaching at all.

Dr. Bricker was a software engineer at several companies, including Boeing, after getting her undergraduate degree from the University of Michigan. After her PhD in computer science at UW, Dr. Bricker held project manager roles before becoming a teacher. Holding this type of position introduced her to the disparities industry has against women in tech.

During her experience, she tried not to notice that very few women worked in the field of computer science. Dr. Bricker explained, "It didn't feel like there could be anything else. So, I might as well accept it. Does that make sense? Like, this is just the way it was. And so why try and make any changes because, you know, I am one out of ten people; I'm going to be the only woman in this room at work. And that was fine until it wasn't." As Dr. Bricker continued working throughout her career, she noticed she was not getting a voice. People wouldn't hear what she said, until someone else said it louder, and then suddenly it was their idea.

"I can visualize the room that I was in where I said [something] about the design that we were working on, [and I was] completely ignored and then some guy said it **and it got adopted**. And I would just have to go, you know...that was just my life...unless I was forceful enough to interrupt people, like push on people in ways I didn't feel comfortable."

Having her ideas stolen like this was a harsh reality of what the industry was like, and how it valued the voice of men over women. This progressed to not only were her ideas not being heard, to where she was doing all of the work without getting the recognition that what she was doing was above her level.

"I was at a company, and I had gotten to a point where I was essentially doing the work that a director at the company would do, but they would not give me the title or the promotion. And they always would come up with some excuses to why that wasn't the case....And that's sort of where it would start to get a little frustrating."

ADVOCATING FOR DIVERSITY TO MAKE AN IMPACT

This frustration of not being rightfully recognized grew and became a turning point in Dr. Bricker's career. After leaving this company, the opportunity to teach in her son's second grade math class came up. This was a chance to teach young students about computer science— potentially future women in computer science—things they would not normally be exposed to at that young an age. A girl in the class became very excited about the subject—so much that she would talk to her family about it and her uncle showed her new projects. Her interest in computer science led her to explore more, and she was always sitting in the front of class, asking questions.

A couple years later, Dr. Bricker checked in with this girl to see if she had been keeping up with computer science. However, she hadn't been—her parents had not continued to strengthen this interest.

"And it was just so heart-wrenching," Dr. Bricker said. "This is something that she had so much energy toward and they just weren't doing anything to encourage it."

Looking at the statistics about women in tech, I saw that although 55 percent of users on Twitter and Facebook are women, the following statistics about makers and leaders are not representative of these numbers:[17]

- 28 percent of proprietary software jobs are held by women

- 11 percent of Fortune 500 executives are women

- 5 percent of tech start-ups are owned by women

It's important for leadership to represent the user group because there would be less assumptions in the products about the users if that was the case. One of my professors said if we wanted to know the culture of a company, look at the CEO. If the CEO is from a tech background, engineers and programmers will be encouraged to explore and invent. If the CEO is from a business background, the company will be more business- and money-oriented. If the leadership is more diverse, there will be a more inclusive community for diversity.

---

17 "The Latest Stats on Women in Tech," The Muse.

What is more surprising than the lack of women in STEM and leadership positions in the tech world is that "82 percent of men believed that companies DO spend enough time addressing diversity." What data is their belief based on? Maybe their companies really do keep talking about diversity—but talking and taking action are different. One can instigate the other, but when no action is taking place, the right talks aren't happening. This is why it is important to continue advocating for diversity in actionable ways.

Another experience showed Dr. Bricker the impact of being exposed to inclusion in computer science. In an introduction to computer programming class, Dr. Bricker introduced herself as being on the committee for diversity and inclusion at UW's computer science department. Even though it was just mentioned for a few moments, when introducing herself and listing three things she was involved in, this made an impact. After the talk, a young woman came up and asked to learn more about diversity in computer science.

This experience changed what Dr. Bricker thought her impact was. It showed her she could change people's perceptions about computer science.

"So, I started really thinking about like, what am I teaching?" Dr. Bricker said. "How am I teaching it? What are the examples I'm using? There is an example that's in the book about BMI [body mass index]. Why are we using that? Right? And what kinds of things could I be presenting to make it feel more equitable?"

Education is a crucial factor in inclusion. People aren't going to know exclusion exists until they are exposed to it, and the way to combat exclusion is by educating each other through intent or practice. Dr. Bricker's practice of making lessons more inclusive by using examples more people are comfortable with may not only have an impact on other educators, but also on the students.

How many people reading this identify with the experience of exclusion? How many don't? There are so many sides to every story. One experience does not devalue the other, but in the next section, see how privilege alters experiences from an inclusive and an exclusive view of the same culture.

THE EXCLUSIVE HUMAN TRAITS THAT MAKE MEN LEADERS AND WOMEN B*TCHES

In preparation for going to India on a study abroad program, my teacher told us to talk to somebody from there. The group I was in talked to two people—a man and a woman from India, both of whom were international students at our university. When questioned about sexism in the industry, the man said it didn't really exist anymore. The woman said we would see it all the time.

Why did these two people have such different perspectives? They came from different parts of India. Regardless, they each would have different experiences of growing up and living in India. However, the experience of many women is the men don't realize or identify the sexism that surrounds them since it isn't something that affects them and impedes their successes in life.

In an article from *The New York Times*, Charles M. Blow wrote about his male privilege:

"I must follow the advice on sexism that I proffer on racism: If you are not actively working to dismantle it, you are supporting it. It is not sufficient to simply not be a sexist yourself if you are a man. You must also recognize that you benefit from the system of sexism in ways to which you may not even be aware." [18]

Through recognition comes learning and being able to identify cases where women are treated unfairly due to sexism. This recognition develops a more inclusive mindset—knowing and identifying the times women's voices are ignored can enable people to do something about it, like speak up. Kate Edwards, who started the Geopolitical Strategy group at Microsoft before creating her own company, Geografy, shared some stories with me that she had seen on a women's-only Facebook group where women told stories of what they'd experienced in the workplace.

"Some of the stories are just horrible. Just horror stories, where there's a woman in a meeting and she's the group leader and then they basically talk her down, or she'll say something and then they ignore it and then a guy later will say the same thing and they're like:

'Oh that's a great idea. That's fantastic. You know you're really smart for coming up with that.'

And she's just like, *'Hey, I said that fifteen minutes ago.'*

---

18   Charles M. Blow, "Checking My Male Privilege," *New York Times*, October 29, 2017.

It's like nobody said anything...they're like:

'Oh you're just— now you're just being...you're trying to claim his idea.'

It's like *'You people didn't listen to me.'*

It is sometimes that blatant where it's that kind of level of ignoring her input...A lot of it comes from the company culture itself when the companies are run mostly by men."

Sexism in the workplace exists in many more forms than this. Even the way women are criticized at work amongst their coworkers is different from the way men are criticized. Ways women are talked down upon do not even apply to their work, but how they look or how assertive they are

Kate Edwards explains, "The industry is criticizing them in a way—but not criticizing them for what they're saying, or what they're thinking. It's criticizing them for how they look...or their attitudes, like *'That woman's a bitch because she's always angry'*...Of course, if a man is like that then the man is assertive, he's bold. Whereas if a woman is like that then she's a bitch and she's aggressive."

This is not the first time I have heard about women being seen as "bitchy" in the workplace. People would never describe a man as being a "bitch" for establishing leadership, but women are often looked down upon for doing the same. Just the fact of their gender determines how they are supposed to be leaders. The Harvard Business Review said "female leaders, much more than their male counterparts, face the need to be warm and nice (what society traditionally expects from women), as well as competent or tough (what society traditionally expects from men and leaders)."[19] This expectation isn't something reflected for both men and women, furthering the need to have an inclusive mind beyond design, but also in workplace culture.

Inclusive design in this case is applicable to the creation of community norms. The millions of sexist stories against women in the workplace confirms the exclusive traits underlying our communities and speaks to the importance of changing them. We are going to change this by being more inclusive in designing a community that welcomes differences and experiences based on what people have done, as opposed to what they look like.

Women—in tech, in business, in leadership positions, everywhere—face discrimination and exclusivity at many levels. Women are the ones forging ahead to make the mountain of gender equality taller and taller, to support the women who come next. As a woman in STEM, I hope to show others we have power and can make an impact through our words and actions. This growth for gender equality isn't linear with the complexities of diversity and religion and personal qualities, but continued advocation and recognition to cultivate inclusion will allow us to move toward an inclusively designed community.

---

19 Wei Zheng et al., "How Women Manage the Gendered Norms of Leadership," *Harvard Business Review,* November 28, 2018.

LET'S INCLUSIFY

- Value everyone's thoughts by listening and understanding.

- Practice understanding the intent behind how you traditionally do things and the audience it is affecting.

- Practice creating a welcoming environment to be inclusive to all.

THE COMPLEXITIES OF ACCESSIBILITY

"A primary focus of accessibility is access by people with disabilities. The larger scope of accessibility includes benefits to people without disabilities."

—BY JIM THATCHER IN CONSTRUCTING ACCESSIBLE WEBSITES [20]

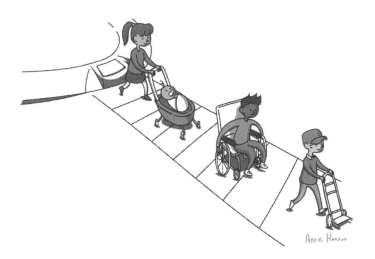

---

20 Jim Thatcher et al., *Constructing Accessible Web Sites* (Apress, 2002).

When I say inclusive design, many people automatically think accessibility. And accessible design, specifically as it pertains to designing for persons with disabilities, is a subset of inclusive design. However, accessibility is often more complicated than discrepancies between people and their built environment—their economic statuses and local resources are some things that can also have an impact.

I first learned about compounded disparities while studying abroad in South Africa with the Rehabilitation department. Our focus was learning about "Disability in Resource Limited Communities." I loved South Africa, from the exciting things to do in Cape Town, the quiet streets of Worcester brightened with fresh oranges that a truck sold by the bag, and the vast rolling hills and beaches opening up to the Indian Ocean in Hobeni, to the incredible mentors we met. These mentors taught us about the different facilities where they took care of people with different disabilities. The underlying theme of all these stories, however, was the complexities regarding optimal access.

One complexity concerned children with disabilities in a home in Hobeni—the home was a safe place for them to grow up and learn, but sometimes their families would take them back to show the government that the child's current address was at their home, so they would receive the supplementary check for that month. When they had the check, they would take the child back to the home for children with disabilities. Is this a good thing or a bad thing? Wouldn't the child be happy to go see their family and stay with them? Wouldn't the child be better taken care of in the home for children with disabilities if their family couldn't take care of them in the first place? What is right?

Laws have been created to support people with disabilities in both the physical and digital worlds. When I asked my professor, Dr. Mankoff, if she had any resources I could use, she told me there were a few books I could check out. A couple days later, she brought down a stack of ten thick books from her office to the cafe where I worked within the computer science building and handed them off to me in a quick pass at the cash register.

One of them, *Designing Accessible Web Sites,* explained how creating websites not accessible for people is exactly what people are not trying to do when creating them. "Shutting out users this way is entirely against the nature and intent of web communication."[21] This statement is also reflected in other work outside of the digital world, such as products and experiences— like being able to do something independently.

The Universal Declaration of Human Rights states that "everyone has the right to freely participate in the cultural life of the community, to enjoy the arts and to share in scientific advancement and its benefits."[22] This becomes an increasingly large issue as we discover many people are facing different types of barriers. The Center of Disease Control states that "one in four US adults—sixty-one million Americans—have a disability that impacts major life activities."[23] This statistic highlights the need for inclusive design to be at the forefront of creation.

---

21   Jeremy Sydik, *Design Accessible Web Sites*: 36 Keys to Creating Content for All Audience and Platforms (Pragmatic Bookshelf, 2007).

22   "The Universal Declaration of Human Rights," Universal Declaration of Human Rights, United Nations.

23   "CDC: 1 in 4 US adults live with a disability," CDC Newsroom, Centers for Disease Control and Prevention.

ENHANCING ABILITIES

"I feel like it's kind of my life's mission to create devices that enhance people's ability to reach their maximum potential," explained Jessica Zistatsis, a mechanical engineer whose work in accessibility made me interested in learning about her experiences.

My friend, Melissa Birchfield, author of *Data for Dignity*, introduced Jessica and me through Facebook. I was interested in talking to her about designing for accessibility and her insights on the subject after earning her master's degree in mechanical engineering at UW. She also co-founded the program HuskyADAPT, an organization on campus that has different groups: one for adapting toys to be more accessible, another for adapting small cars for specific children, and the third for allowing students to get exposure doing various projects about accessibility.

Currently, Jessica is a mechanical engineer and quality manager at Orthocare Innovations. When I asked her about inclusive design, she explained her role in designing for accessibility. "My work is a lot about rehabilitation devices... basically: *'How can I equip a person to better navigate their environment,'* instead of *'How do I design the environment to accommodate people who have different abilities.'*"

An example Jessica uses to explain this concept is based on a project students completed in HuskyADAPT, where they designed a device that allowed a woman with muscle weakness to brush her teeth independently. After her stroke, she was no longer able to brush her teeth and relied on her husband to help her. The students then designed a device that would allow her to independently brush her teeth by creating a holder that compensates for the differences in what hand position is comfortable and the position the toothbrush needs to be in to brush teeth. This kind of design makes the physical world a more inclusive space.

Tools that enable people with physical impairments to do things they want to do allow them to become more independent. Orthocare Innovations has created an app that allows people to change the position of their prosthetic limb so it can adapt to different contexts. The decision to create this kind of feature was informed by the work of engineers and clinical researchers.

"We spend a lot of time working with engineers, but we have a CEO who is a certified prosthetist, and he practiced for many years before becoming CEO," Jessica explained. "And then we have a part-time researcher. So she works at a clinic, seeing amputees with prosthetics and then she works in our office to help inform our design, but it's clinically relevant to give us feedback on like, 'Yeah, that looks really cool but nobody's gonna wear that because of XYZ.' So we have a kind of innovation and clinical relevance on our team."

Having people of different backgrounds on a team can improve the success of designing for inclusion. With each of their backgrounds, they can provide insights based off of research or build things the other team members might not have been able to.

"So, when the clinician is prescribed the device...they set it up a certain way for a certain situation. But then the patient is going to go home and put on different shoes and do other things so they need to have some level of stability on their own. They don't have to go into the clinic every time they want to get adjusted."

The user being able to adjust their device themselves gives them power and freedom. The freedom of controlling their device to make it do what they want is a crucial level of independence important also for mental health. Everyone wants to have some control over their lives. If tools are designed appropriately to fit the person's lifestyle, they will regain the independence and live life the way they want to. Jessica explains why they found the need for an app to adjust the prosthetic during use:

"People change on a day-to-day basis, even throughout the day...We want to wear high-heeled shoes. And then switch into tennis shoes later," Jessica explained. Changing into different shoes requires the ankle to be in a different position—and if that position isn't changed, then the person will walk differently. This can "cause joint paint and other secondary issues." Jessica said.

By having this app, which adjusts the position of the prosthetic, it is safer for the user in the long term because it can prevent injuries. If they try to do things during their day that are not what the prosthetic device is prepared to handle, it can, in the long term, negatively affect other parts of their body. For example, weightlifting. On a machine where your feet are supposed to be angled a certain way, it is important to have that angle when pushing out from your feet because it is putting the strain on the correct muscles; however, if a person does this repeatedly with their feet pointing straight up, it has the potential to harm their body in the long run. The app Orthocare created allows users to participate in their daily norms with the correct positions for their prosthetics.

This means their prosthetic will allow them to participate in different opportunities—becoming not a rigid solution, but a flexible tool, reflecting the constantly changing environments we enter each day. This shows inclusion because it incorporates other aspects of someone's life—it is inclusive of a lifestyle, as opposed to a single moment.

In addition to partaking in different activities during the day, there are other practical reasons for this ability. Jessica's example shows that negative health effects can be caused by rigid prosthetics. With prosthetics, there is a socket that connects the prosthetic to the residual limb (the remaining part of the limb that is missing). This socket is custom made to fit that person. However, our bodies do not constantly stay the same—they change over time due to external forces.

"As it gets hotter outside, your fingers might swell, your body gets larger, volume fluctuates. And then if you're really cold, your limbs tend to shrink a little bit," Jessica explained. "That happens in a prosthetic as well. And once your leg is a different size, it doesn't fit as well into that rigid socket...we created a vacuum system to dynamically adjust its volume to the volume of the residual limb so it's always going to fit. So we need a patient app for that, where they can say *'Oh hey you know I'm going to be walking really fast but I need a tighter vacuum,'* or, *'I'm going to be going into the water so I need to shut off the pump.'* It's how they can better engage in daily life."

The devices that Orthocare Innovations makes are really cool, and they are helping people take control of their life; however, there are constraints the engineers and designers at Orthocare need to work with, and that is money. They need to design products within the budget for the specific user group, otherwise othe user group would not have access to these designs. Due to this constraint, different aspects of the design need to be considered under this light. Through disregarding the economic status of their users, technologies can become unfeasible for a large amount of people, even if it could be super helpful to them at certain times.

For example, diabetes medicine: there is a shot that works well for my mom. The medicine is not only alleviating the immediate symptoms of diabetes, but is helping her become healthier. In a few months, she might be able to go off of diabetes treatment entirely because of the positive effects of this one medicine. But after a month of getting insurance coverage for this medication, the insurance company decided they weren't going to pay for it anymore. Now, they will only cover insulin. If my mom starts taking insulin, she will not be able to stop for the rest of her life. The optimal medicine is $1,000 in the United States, even though it is hundreds of dollars cheaper in Canada, just a three-hour drive away.

To design for users who rely on insurance, Jessica said, "[We] have to do market research and see what the number of people in the US, Europe, etc. that are eligible is. And based off that market size, and Medicare's reimbursement value of the proposed product, we have to determine if it is even worth us developing the product."

When I asked what it meant for someone to be eligible, Jessica explained to me different factors that needed to be considered, such as:

- How sensitive is their skin tissue?

- What other medical complications do they have?

- How active are they?

- What is their mobility level? (i.e. can the person walk independently, would they be able to run if given the appropriate technology, do they need other assistive devices like a cane, walker, etc.)

"Do some background research and try to quantify [it]," Jessica said. "Obviously it's all an estimate but you kind of have to look at it. What's the big picture market? And then, what part of that market can we actually address?"

Setting constraints, based both on money and ability, can be a really hard process to navigate. If one user group is being included, another might be excluded. Additionally, on some level, money and affordability is also part of those decisions. So then what? Should there be one improved solution for the rich and a subpar solution for the poor?

One person challenging this issue is Nicole Ver Kuilen. She is advocating to improve the standard of care for amputees through her nonprofit organization, Forrest Stump.[24] On her

24 "Why Forrest Stump?" Forrest Stump, accessed on June 4th, 2020.

website, Nicole explains the barriers she faced in receiving prosthetics: "First, a waterproof limb was considered a 'convenience item' and denied by insurance. Later, a leg built for running was deemed 'not medically necessary'."[24] The only prosthetic insurance will give Nicole is "designed only for walking."[24]

We do not have to sacrifice quality—constraints can be both very frustrating in the moment when trying to create within them, but they can also lead to innovative and creative solutions, resulting in a better product also inclusive for different abilities and economic statuses.

What impressed me most about what Jessica does is how Orthocare is designing for the flexibility of everyday human life, enabling clients to more freely participate in experiences, as is their human right.[22] Their considerations not only include physical ability and utilizing innovations in technology (such as connecting apps to prosthetic devices), but also the affordability of their products, relating to the sentiment from *Designing Accessible Web Sites*, and making sure users have access to the experience.

This demonstrates the intersectionality of inclusion, which considers both accessibility and economic status. Another story that explores this intersection is from a conversation I had with Lynsay Whelan, an occupational therapist I connected with previously.

INCLUSIFYING INDEPENDENCE

Through HuskyADAPT, I worked on a research project about e-NABLE, a nonprofit that has open source 3D-printed prosthetic models which volunteers can 3D print and send to people, usually for free. During this project, I interviewed prosthetic makers in the US and was connected with Lynsay. I was excited to reach out to her again for this book because of her experience volunteering abroad. Lynsay is an occupational therapist who has spent time in Iraq through the army and currently works at a prosthetic company. She has also volunteered abroad in Ukraine and Tanzania.

To begin, an occupational therapist is someone who helps somebody gain more independence through their daily life, whether it be getting dressed, going to school, or cooking. The occupational therapist sees if they can adapt the environment, activity, or create a tool that can increase that person's independence. Lynsay described it as a "very unique profession in that it looks holistically at the person and their environment to help them live life to the fullest. OTs help their clients be as independent as possible, regardless of any physical, mental, or psychosocial challenges they may experience."

A woman who had lost both of her arms at the elbow from a bus accident in Tanzania is a story that stuck with me for months, prompting me to talk to Lynsay again. Due to this accident, for fourteen years, the woman could not go to the bathroom by herself or feed herself without help. This loss of independence, after being independent throughout her adult life—and even being depended on by her daughters as she raised them—must have been shocking. To help her regain control in some parts of her everyday life, Lynsay, along with local physiotherapists, created a solution together.

One of the first things they examined was how, culturally, people went to the bathroom.

"[Something] to keep in mind is culturally they don't use toilet paper there," Lynsay said. "They don't have bathrooms in their homes. So it's a neighborhood bathroom. And so you have to leave your home, go down the road to [an] outhouse-style bathroom, and then [the solution] needed to be something that was easy enough to move so that everyone in the neighborhood using this [bathroom] didn't have to use the system, but that [she could] easily get it in place by herself."

It is important to consider culture. If Lynsay had just mailed them a bidet that we would find in the United States, there is no way it would have worked with the community-style bathrooms the neighborhood has! Being present in the environment with the user makes innovations like these happen. The constraints were not only the physical constraints of how to make a bidet this woman could use, but also one she would be able to move around using tools that were already there.

Lynsay explained that they "took a lawn chair and this hose and a bucket and cut a hole out of the seat of the lawn chair... [and] the handle that she was using was just a two-by-four attached to the lawn chair. She could actually hit that little handle with her residual limb and then that sprayed the water so that it was just like a little homemade bidet."

In addition to making this bidet, they also created something the woman could strap onto her residual limb so she could feed herself and brush her teeth. This was made with just a piece of Velcro containing a slit and a D-ring—and now she does not need to wait for one of her two daughters to help her eat.

Another important aspect of this adaption was using materials available in their environment.

"The concept was to use locally available materials to create the solution. The benefit being that if they needed to adapt something, or if it broke, it could be fixed without relying on materials brought from the United States."

The aspects of inclusion crucial to take away from this example were how the occupational therapists needed to not only understand how things worked in the local environment, but also what was present in that environment.

Delivering a Westernized solution and just leaving it with the user in Tanzania might be fine for a while, but as soon as something doesn't work or a piece of it breaks, the whole device is useless and the user reverts back to their previous lifestyle, living with the same pain points as before. Adapting the local resources ensures that people there will be able to fix the portable bidet and adapt it over time as necessary. The ability to fix and maintain the bidet makes it a more inclusive solution and ensures long-term independence, which can be considered a top goal in inclusive design.

In order to find solutions, however, they needed to know what the problems were in the context of the woman's daily life. This is how Lynsay finds those pain points:

"I would just have some kind of interview with the person and ask them:

- What do you find challenging throughout your day-to-day life?

- Is there anything you currently can't do that you want to be able to do?

And we're just kind of talking to people about their day and what sort of challenges they encounter and then after that, if it was something that there's already some kind of solution for...we could either use that or, if it wasn't available locally, try to recreate it with locally available materials."

By understanding the person's environment, the occupational therapists can make useful adaptions. If they don't, they lack lasting impact.

Lynsay said, "There was the interview process where I was working with local physiotherapists, [since] they knew the culture more, but for me, one thing that was interesting was to better understand...toileting. I have a little toolbox full of ideas of what I would normally do with someone in the United States. But, you know, my next question was, *'What can you tell me about the bathroom that you're in?'* And you know, that's when I really learned a lot about, *'Oh, wait, you don't even have it in your house. You have to go down the road and know how it was set up.'* So just really kind of understanding someone's environment and understanding some of the challenges was helpful for me."

This is user experience research, since they looked at the experience the woman had in her daily life, which then informed their design decisions. To learn about a person's environment, Lynsay finds it useful to go to the person's home or even just see pictures of their home or environment to understand it better.

Lynsay's story exemplifies how constraints—in this case, limited resources—can create inclusive solutions that work well in the environment the user is in. Additionally, we can make independence inclusive. The goal of accessible design is to allow people to do things on their own. This might be brushing their teeth after an arm amputation or getting around a city in a wheelchair. There are many ways to develop an inclusive society...creating inclusive physical experiences is one of them.

LETS INCLUSIFY

- Practice exploring the physical and cultural environments that your product will be used in.

- If you can't go and expose yourself to the user environment, practice finding other ways to understand the environment.

- Practice using local materials in the context of users to promote a sustainable product life cycle.

AGEISM, A BACKWARDS PHENOMENON

"Discrimination on the basis of age is as unacceptable as discrimination on the basis of any other aspect of ourselves that we cannot change."

—ASHTON APPLEWHITE[25]

---

25 Ashton Applewhite, *This Chair Rocks: A Manifesto Against Ageism,* (Networked Books, 2016).

Another way to develop an inclusive society is by cultivating an inclusive environment that welcomes all people despite differences. One of those differences might be age. Discrimination against people based on age has become prevalent amongst industries, which is strange because of the media stereotype correlating wisdom and age.

Any story arc would be incomplete without a mentor. Gandalf (*The Lord of the Rings*), Splinter (*Teenage Mutant Ninja Turtles*), Obi-Wan Kenobi (*Star Wars*), and Mr. Miyagi (*The Karate Kid*) are all typical mentor figures we think of. They provided wisdom and guidance to the heroes of the stories. Their accomplishments are in the past, and now the accomplishments of their mentees is what is highlighted. However, this in itself is not reflective of people working in the industry today. In real life—while mentors are still important—people over the age of fifty do a lot more than mentor. In fact, they do all the same things they did (and others do) before they had hit fifty. The ideas and innovation and creation doesn't suddenly stop, so why then are people labeled as "old" facing ageism?

The phenomenon of ageism is defined by the WHO as "the stereotyping, prejudice, and discrimination against people on the basis of their age."[26]

IN THE WORKPLACE

This illegal form of discrimination perseveres throughout the national workforce, as shown by these statistics from the American Association for Retired Persons:[27]

---

26 "Ageism," Ageing and Life-course, World Health Organization.

27 Joe Kita, "Workplace Age Discrimination Still Flourishes in America," *AARP*, December 30, 2019.

- 25 percent of workers age forty-five and older have been subjected to negative comments about their age from supervisors or coworkers.

- 60 percent of older workers have seen or experienced age discrimination in the workplace.

- 7 percent of these older workers see age discrimination as a hurdle to finding a new job; another report found that more than half of these older workers are prematurely pushed out of longtime jobs and 90 percent of them never earn as much again.

Reading through the comments on Joe Kita's article, "Workplace Age Discrimination Still Flourishes in America," shocked me. People of old age were sharing their stories of how their managers, who had become their friends, didn't even support them. They were talking about their struggles in finding new jobs and being treated unfairly based off their age and not on their work ethic. There are so many stories like these out there. In order to prevent those stories from becoming our own, or our parents', we need to seriously evaluate the decisions being made and examine what injustices people are facing due to ageism.

I grew up with the adage, "respect your elders." However, this saying does not seem to be reciprocated in the tech industry. From Matt Asay's article "Jimmy Wales to Silicon Valley: Grow up and Get over Your Age Bias," I learned it may be because we keep hearing stories about how young people are creating all of these successful start-ups and believe this is what the start-up scene looks like.[28]

---

28 Matt Asay, "Jimmy Wales to Silicon Valley: Grow up and Get over Your Age Bias," *readwrite*, September 27, 2013.

"All of us in Silicon Valley—business people, investors, reporters, but especially impatient young entrepreneurs—fetishize start-ups today. We obsess about technology and products. We tell the Steve Jobs story, the Mark Zuckerberg story, the Bill Gates story, over and over again....We look at success and see only the short half of the picture." [28]

I have also experienced this. I keep hearing the same stories about the people who created the top three largest internationally-known corporations. But they aren't the only ones out there. Asay's article also goes on to list different people that have had their big break in their forties or fifties, such as the creators of Intel, Zipcar, and Craigslist. This trend hasn't suddenly disappeared with young people creating start-ups.

"The highest rate of entrepreneurship in America has shifted to the fifty-five to sixty-four age group, with people over fifty-five almost twice as likely to found successful companies than those between twenty and thirty-four." [28]

Looking at these different types of examples exposes how misinformed our society's assumption that start-ups are only created and run by young professionals is. The danger of this assumption is that now we are facing this ageism phenomenon, and it is stunting our growth and innovation in the long run.

I had never challenged my assumptions of what I had imagined a start-up to look like, which was the image of a college graduate getting funding and hiring their other college graduate friends to put a team together. What challenged this assumption was my meeting with Kate Edwards.

Before I heard Kate Edwards speak in Advanced Communications in HCDE—which had an emphasis on UX and Globalization—my professor sent a link of Kate Edward's Wikipedia page to the class so we could learn more about her before her talk. I was impressed to see she had won a particular award: Top Fifty over Fifty in the Gaming Industry. Digging deeper, I learned that she had created the award to combat ageism in the tech industry.

When I asked Kate about ageism, she started out with giving me a statistic that there are more women gaming in their thirties and forties than there are teen males gaming. This just confirms that having "older" people in the gaming industry would be more representative of the demographic of videogame players.

"I started this Fifty over Fifty list a couple years ago because...I see that Forbes has the Thirty under Thirty list every year [and] they just released one for the game industry in the last three decades," Kate explained. "And it's great...I know a lot of people on the list. I'm very happy for them. I'm very proud of them, because they are really talented people. But to me, all that does is double down on the youth culture and highlight the fact that our society values [youth] over age and experience....There's an incredible amount of talent out there who are in their older years, who are just wasted because these youth oriented tech industries just don't value them."

Something I thought about when hearing this was the fact that there are thousands of engineers going into tech in the greater Seattle area. There are even more in areas of California, and the places we associate as being tech hubs are expanding and new ones are popping up in more places. Most of these younger engineers are not necessarily inventing something new and shiny—they are creating products built from the foundation of various programming languages and tools that have already been built by the previous generation of engineers and designers. This shows it is important to value people that have been in the industry a long time because they have already seen and tested these things and can guide processes accordingly. However, because of the exclusive age bubble surrounding innovation and technology, it has created an issue not reflected in other communities.

Kate explained that this problem of ageism in the gaming industry is actually mainly a problem within our society, especially because some cultures in East Asia and indigenous communities still highly respect the wisdom of their elders, which is unlike what she sees here in our Western society.

"I think a lot of this is...a kind of more modern developed country phenomenon...it's because [in] a lot of traditional cultures, a lot of cultures that have been around for millennia, elderly people are given a lot more, I think value, than we tend to see in Western countries." said Kate.

It is interesting that Kate notes how this trait of ageism in society is not reflected in the media we are exposed to.

"We see it all the time and [in] all of these fictional narratives that we enjoy, and yet we don't for some reason carry over that same value to the real world. So it's like, where's the Gandalf, Dumbledore, or Yodas, in our world? All around us there's amazing people who are older, who have the experience and the perspective."

Some ways to be inclusive of people who are older in the workplace are:

- **Accessible team building.** Make sure to be cognizant of what barriers team building activities might have, whether they are ice breakers when someone joins the team, or outings for people to get to know each other.

- **Flexible workplace environment.** Create a workplace environment that is flexible to adapt to people's needs, whether physical (is it easy to get around the office, or do people need to navigate amongst many desks?), or environmental (can people change the temperature of the office? Is it possible to work remotely?).

You might notice these suggestions would be nice overall. That is one benefit of being inclusive—although we are forced to think more creatively, there are positive benefits for all people involved!

DEMOGRAPHIC PROJECTIONS

Another implication of ageism is how it ties into disability. As we get older, there is a higher possibility of developing visual impairments and decreases of mobility, among other challenges. Taking this into consideration, the statistic from the "Projections of the Size and Composition of the US Population: 2014 to 2060 " that "the older population is projected to more than double in size from 46 million to 98 million over this period [2014 to 2060]" reinforces the need to make products and experiences with accessibility in mind.[29]

29   Sandra L. Colby and Jennifer M Ortman, "Projections of the Size and Composition of the US Population: 2014 to 2060," *United States Census Bureau,* March 2015.

This same document, which analyzes population growth, explains that diversity of the older generation is also going to increase a lot. "For the oldest age group, those sixty-five and over, the foreign-born population is expected to nearly double its share, increasing from 13 percent in 2014 to 26 percent in 2060." 29 These numbers reinforce the need to be inclusive of diversity and ability. We, as makers, should be challenged to create accessibly for all so that everyone has the opportunity to remain contributors to society and participators in life.

Something to remember from this is that everybody's experience is valid. Just because somebody did not grow up in a certain social world does not mean they do not know about it. Each generation of people is not suddenly removed from "society"—they have lived it in a different way with previous experiences that give them different perspectives on what is happening. The more diverse the perspectives that influence design, the stronger the product has the potential to be. Strength through diversity is directly connected to inclusive design because the diversity in people involved is what can influence a group of people to think more inclusively.

LET'S INCLUSIFY

- Be aware of how you think of your co-workers on the basis of age and practice questioning why you think that way.

- Practice looking at people based on what you know about them, not what stereotypes tell you about them.

A COMPARISON BETWEEN DESIGN AND POLITICS

"Nothing about us, without us."

—MICHAEL MASUTHA

Imagine this: you're a farmer in the outskirts of Bangalore, a quickly growing city with a population of twelve million people. You have a quiet life, with the exception of the birds that are always singing in the forest around you. You know there are leopards, but your family has been there for generations, so you don't feel fear as you lead your cows through the forest to your grazing land.

Fast forward two years, and you are again leading your cows through the forest. The bird song fades as the noise of traffic emanates from the newly-built highway. You emerge from the forest with your cows. The churning vehicle engines and the honking overwhelm your senses. You can see the cow's grazing spot across the five-lane highway that now circles around the city, then you begin walking along it to the tunnel that is ten kilometers down the road. This is the only safe place for your cows to cross. You knew they were going to put the highway in, but what were you going to do? The authorities did what was convenient for them.

I learned about this story from Bhargavi (Bar-ga-vee) Rao, a mentor I met through a study abroad program in India. After working in environmental science and microbiology, she found that her passion lies more with public policy and social justice work. Sitting in labs researching how to cure diseases or sickness was not enough—she wanted to find out how she could stop those from happening in the first place.

Bhargavi brought up two points that led her to determine that her impact should be at the source: one, stopping the problem at the source would prevent people from getting ill, and two, it would be a lot cheaper for the government to invest in work to stop these problems rather than using their money to put a Band-Aid on the problem. Unfortunately, vaccines are expensive. When most of the people suffering are from rural or low economic environments, will they be able to pay for medicine, even when the cause of the illness still exists and can strike again?

This thought process can be applied to inclusion as well. One, people are being excluded and unable to participate in experiences because they were not included in the process at the source of design. Many times adaptions are designed later as opposed to designing more inclusive products initially. And two, companies would not only save money from not having to develop adaptions, but they would increase the amount of people that can use their products.

Bhargavi identified policy as something that can initiate a change in the system to provide clean water, and so she decided to pursue law. She's like a scientist and a lawyer all in one.

It was interesting to hear from her in class, so I approached her during a trip to a village outside of Bangalore. On a quiet morning, we walked along the banks of a beautiful river until we found a table where we could sit. The greenery and sparkling sun made the river enticing in the hot weather, but knowing that sewage was dumped directly in it prevented any students in our program from going in. A small boy in Disney *Cars*-themed crocs splashed in the steps of the water, however, his dad watching close by. Small fallen leaves sprinkled over the top of the table with little bugs crawling along them, and I pushed them off so I could put my notebook down.

Within minutes they came back and I needed to take care not to squish anything while I was writing. After we were settled, she told me stories—stories about how politics have affected waste and how people with lower economic status have been affected by the top-down approach the country has ended up adopting.

Bhargavi's efforts in raising awareness of the power people have from the Constitution of India have changed communities for the better. Showing people that they have a voice leads them to feel empowered to pressure their local government, which in turn can help create changes within their local community. This demonstrates the cruciality of incorporating the stakeholders in the beginning of any design process, whether it is design of communities or of products.

Decisions that lead to damaging consequences for communities are made by a group of people who do not represent the people they are affecting. "Who are they making a part of this decision-making? Why are the communities who come particularly from low-income neighborhoods, or other castes and classes, religion-based communities, been kept away from many of these decision-making issues?" Bhargavi asked. These decision makers either don't care or don't know because they don't deal with the consequences.

"They are not accountable to the people," Bhargavi said. "And they don't care who wants what they conduct, no public consultations, no nothing."

This lack of representation in political decisions affecting communities is reflected in the design world. In previous chapters, we have seen that women are not represented in leadership roles of industries women are users in—there are so many more places with a lack of diversity, even though there is diversity of users. One paper examining the lack of diversity in biomedical studies pinpointed that the lack of diversity in the researchers was the reason for this problem.

"One answer can be found in the reluctance of minority group members to participate in biomedical research or clinical trials. This reluctance is accentuated when few of the scientists doing the research or running the trials are themselves members of minority groups." [30]

Where does this reluctance come from? Maybe it has to do with culture or identity—feeling comfortable that we will be understood or trusting the researchers to understand where we come from. This theme of not participating where we are not represented is seen throughout all industries.

The biggest way to combat making things that exclude people is to have diversity in the makers themselves, because then the perspectives of diverse backgrounds flow into broadening the scope of considered users.

The organization Bhargavi worked with to increase inclusion when making decisions is not seeing much change.

"We've always, you know, seen who they have invited and pointed out, '*They* have missed out and *they* have missed out,' and [the government officials] will give some lame reason. So, we say that if [the stakeholders] are not at this, the meeting should not happen. Naturally they postpone. So, we've always lobbied and advocated for a very inclusive participation from everybody." Bhargavi explained.

Despite trying to get inclusion at this level, of including the people who will be affected at the government level, they still do not see more inclusion happening—and Bhargavi knows why. It is because of the current top-down approach, which is excluding the people it is supposed to be supporting.

Bhargavi has no hope for a top-down approach to change the system. "It is only from a bottom-up is what's going to make our cities inclusive. See, in most Indian neighborhoods, we all live in very [diverse] neighborhoods. I will have people from North India, South India, people speaking different languages, different religions, cultures living with me. So, in a top-down approach, what happens if I'm a Brahmin, if I'm a Hindu, Kannada-speaking, I will probably get selected by the authorities to come and participate in a meeting. And especially if I'm a businesswoman...I will get easily selected."

When I asked how this exclusion at decision-making meetings could be changed, Bhargavi's response was, "Educating the general community about law."

> Education about inclusive design is what will make an impact. People need to know how they can design inclusively in order to do it. Once they start designing inclusively, it is something other people might start thinking about and then begin doing over time.

Bhargavi gave me an example of when this bottom-up approach worked:

There was a community in northern Bangalore, near the airport, and a landfill was built where they live. The community knew it was going to happen, but due to India's history with colonization, people were used to being told what was going to happen, with no power to stop it.

"It was the grazing pasture and lands and [the landfill became] contaminated and everything else became impossible—livelihoods became impossible. People could no longer practice agriculture. Whole lot of problems. So that's when we said, *'Okay, why [don't we] teach them how to start off with fighting the law?'* But...they need to understand what their rights are. And how our system of governance will [work]. We did a lot of workshops, not just environmental legal provisions, but also of local governance. And today that government is taking care of their problems completely. They completely shut down the landfill."

I love this example because it shows how much power people have when they rise up and fight back. They have a right to do it. The interesting thing is that the constitution has laws to incorporate inclusion, since India is such an incredibly diverse place. Diversity in religion, in language, in socio-economic status, in castes. The people who wrote India's constitution thought about these people, and how to be inclusive toward them and make sure they were not ignored and stepped on.

"The constitution has special provisions. It has special provisions for people who come from minority religions, minority backgrounds, [but it's] a whole lot of rubbish...as we are not paying enough attention to all of that. We don't live by that."

So what happened? Their implementation lacked representation of the users, leaving many without knowledge of their rights and no one accountable to the constitution.

IMPLEMENTING WITH THE USER

Designing with the user is an important aspect of inclusive design, because otherwise there is a chance of people being left out or assumptions being made about the users. However, implementing with the user is just as crucial. One way to do this is by having a diverse leadership team.

Sylvester Renner once wrote, "The ripple effect of having diverse representation in leadership is immense. Young girls can be inspired that they are up to the task in any industry vertical; the disabled will know there are no boundaries they can't overcome; people from different races and religion will know they are valued in the society."[30] This is confirmed by the statistics of women working for Kaiser Permanente: "Kaiser Permanente's workforce is so diverse that there is no racial majority. The company is also three-quarters female, with many women in top positions. One-third of Kaiser's physicians are women, as are nearly half of its executives and more than 35 percent of its board of directors."[31]

Bangalore did this by organizing themselves to allow for communities to have a voice in what happens to them. The way government is organized in Bangalore is this: under the state government is the local governments, and under the local governments there are hundreds of wards, which are composed of local communities. The local government is responsible for being some sort of liaison between the wards and the state government.

The local government comes to a ward with what the state government wants to do, and the ward will look over these plans and comment on them and make decisions to change things if needed, so that those plans can be beneficial to the current community.

"So, all the plans there are consolidate. And that plan is given to the state government saying that these are the plans for the city. *'Every ward has come out with its own plan, please have a look at it and approve it and whatever finances is required.'*"

However, this has not been practiced because those in power go around the voice of their citizens by hiring para-statal agencies.

These parastatal agencies are not responsible for prioritizing the local communities, so they will plan to cater to their boss—the people in power, who as mentioned before, are not representative of the people they are leading. They don't even know what is going on at the ward level. However, the government goes to use these parastatal agencies because "it becomes easier for them to implement the project. Less involvement from people, less resistance, fewer questions. And it's a very top-down approach." This has been a problem since soon after India became independent, despite the constitution.

Who is being catered to now, in our design world? And how do we change that? I believe the best way to inclusify experiences and products and our society is to make people aware of just how exclusive it is now, and what other people are doing to change it. Bhargavi even said that in order to fix the challenges India is facing right now, "awareness is what is required. And that is what will make societies more inclusive," and that "lack of awareness can lead to all sorts of discrimination. Even some...unknowing people can get discriminated [against]."

Incorporating users early into the design process is only going to happen if companies become more aware of why it is important to do so. Currently though, I think the biggest barrier is convincing the people in power that it is important, not only for social good but also for increasing profits, which is not necessarily something that should be a top priority for those actually doing the research and designing and creating, but from what I have learned on the journey of writing this book, profit is a top priority for those in power.

STUCK IN THE CYCLE

The cycle of compounded disparities is brutal when it seems like everything is set against you. For example, if you are poor you cannot go to school to get a better job, you keep doing the same job, barely scraping by. And even with enough financial aid to go to school, what if you have other responsibilities? Like a family? Even though you are poor, you are still making enough to scrape by and keep things going, but you can't stop making money to pursue a degree because you are the only source of income. It is hard to break out of this exclusive cycle, both in design and for the socially oppressed.

There are so many ways people identify others: social standing, race, education, and religion. Identifying people in this way feels natural, but these labels are also used to determine what they can or cannot do—or what they are or aren't. When systems or products ignore these differences, exclusion happens and the cycle begins again.

"So then," Bhargavi said. "Trickle-down further generations also stay in the same mental oppression state. And it's pretty much because of the government. It's largely because of the government."

The government has such a big role in this oppression because of how they are controlling the way things are created and implemented—as in, who they are including in that process and who they aren't.

To start breaking out of this cycle, the cycle must be identified and exposed.

EXPOSE YOURSELF TO IT

You can make a change by exposing yourself to the exclusion, which will lead you to recognize disparity in other experiences. Exposing yourself to things not typically in your comfort zone can broaden your perspectives on other experiences. Bhargavi started doing this in school, when she recognized that some of her friends were unwilling to go out as often as others because of how much money they spent. She didn't just randomly come to this conclusion, though—she watched her parents' awareness of exclusion and how they acted against it and was also inspired by the volunteer work she had done through school.

"It is all somewhere, how you grow up and what you're exposed to that matters. So I think it was my parents who had made everything very inclusive. In the very beginning, they would recognize Muslim neighbors and greet them, feed them. I grew up in a Christian institution all my life. So back again, in most of the Christian institutions, you're exposed to a whole lot of the community-related work...and that helps to open your eyes to everything that's happening in the society."

These types of experiences helped keep Bhargavi's eyes open to exclusion and her heart ready to help. When some of her classmates turned down going to fancy dinners or new movies in the theater, Bhargavi chose to stay back and look for things they could all participate in that were free, which ended up being more rewarding memories. Creating inclusive experiences was not the easy route, but having a different solution worked out better since they were able to bond more and experience things together.

Recognizing exclusion in experiences is different than trying to understand them yourself, which is something that seems to happen frequently in the design world. Just because you understand that other people's experiences lead to their different perspectives does not mean your attempts to adopt those differences yourself will give you the ability to understand that perspective. Assumptions factor into it, and the short amount of time during which you adopt that different experience will not transform you. An example people may commonly know is to put on a blindfold and do something while pretending you are blind to test an idea. Instead of adopting this experience, people can try to understand through being exposed to the experience with somebody with visual impairments, instead of as someone with visual impairments.

I practiced exposing myself to different experiences by joining the club HuskyADAPT and adapting toys for accessible play. I realized there are so many ways that interactive toys can be exclusive, especially if the way the toy is designed to be played with is not inclusive to all abilities. However, it was important for me to note that even though I learned how to make toys more accessible for certain abilities, by interacting with the toys through the switches or buttons myself, I was still not getting the same exact experience interacting with it—as an adult person without a disability—compared to a child with a disability.

So, if I were to go a step further to research how fun it is to play with an adapted toy, I wouldn't give myself metrics and test them—I would test those metrics with children who have disabilities. The inaccurate data I would have received through testing myself might have led to design decisions not really based off of the user's experience, which would have resulted in even more exclusion.

To learn more about other experiences and perspectives, practice being curious and learning from others. This way, the people you are designing for can be included, and will know what you create is intentional.

BE CURIOUS

Curiosity is exciting and opens doors to new worlds we didn't even know existed. But it's hard, and sometimes I wonder how I can become more curious. I firmly believe that curiosity is a fundamental necessity for creativity, because creativity starts with "I wonder if..." in your mind. Being curious will compel people to understand other experiences, to seek the boundaries of creativity, and fuel the process of problem solving in innovative ways.

Bhargavi needed to train herself to become more curious as an adult, even when curiosity came so much easier when she was a child. However, forcing herself to keep asking questions is what led her to pursue research to stop the symptoms of things like diarrhea by analyzing the source as opposed to finding a cure that would be too expensive for most people to use anyway.

"You definitely can't solve all of it, but...engage in a discussion about it, talk about it, and try and keep pushing," Bhargavi said. "And even if you don't succeed in doing something, at least it's slowing down the process."

By understanding the cycle of exclusion and seeking ways to expose ourselves and learn about exclusion, we can build programs and products more inclusively. Inclusive design is a huge multi-faceted world with numerous aspects to pursue in terms of creativity and problem solving. By encouraging yourself to learn about at least some facets and opening yourself up to curiosity about things different from your understanding of normalcy, this will help make the shift from our exclusive society to an inclusive one.

LET'S INCLUSIFY
- The practice of excluding users from the making processes might lead to the product having negative consequences on the users.

- Practice working with users to fully understand their needs.

- Seek ways to expose yourself to understanding different experiences—without necessarily simulating the exact experience yourself.

- Exercise your inclusive mind by practicing being curious about how others experience what you do.

LET'S TALK BUSINESS

"Retrofitting always costs more."

—JOE CLARK[30]

---

30   Joe Clark, *Building Accessible Websites* (New Riders Press, 2002).

In Seattle, we are surrounded by tech. Filling the spaces between the Amazon, Facebook, and Airbnb office buildings are hundreds of start-ups creating different forms of new technology. A quote from *Constructing Accessible Websites* explains that "the explosive growth of electronic commerce continues to erect new barriers."[31] This quote exemplifies the need for the adoption of inclusive design in the workflow of these new creations.

Exclusion is something everyone faces in various forms, but feeling empathy for other people is not enough to change the ways of for-profit companies. Those organizations need to see profit in doing the research for diverse users in order to motivate the integration of inclusion into new designs for products or services.

Even thinking about how to make a company change its values of inclusion (or in some cases, start sticking to them) seems overwhelming.

One successful case of a business incorporating inclusive design is Zappos.com. Allie Thu, a technologist at Zappos, spent a year building and raising awareness around inclusive design at the customer service company. Her work ultimately led her to pursue a career path in accessibility. While her experience shows that thinking inclusively on the company level requires passionate work and determination, it also proves how rewarding the outcome can be.

Here's how Allie's personal journey started. On the outskirts of a conference table, she listened to speakers at Amazon's

---

31   Jim Thatcher et al., *Constructing Accessible Web Sites* (Apress, 2002).

annual accessibility summit. The people talking were diverse in job positions and ability. This is where Allie's eyes were opened to the broad world of accessibility and what it can become. She became determined to pursue an inclusive design path at Zappos.

"[I got] a glimpse into a whole world of work that I never really had considered in the past," Allie said. "In regard to navigating our website, we just never thought about people who might not have great vision or be blind or be deaf or have mobility issues or whatever it might be. And that really touched my heart."

She began asking questions like:

- "Where do we currently stand today?"

- "How do we get started?"

- "How can I work on this while also doing my current job?"

Allie split her career between design and programming. After starting in design, she transitioned to front end development. She found her passion between these two career paths, where she understands the technical side of things but enjoys designing and creation.

This set her up well to singlehandedly kickstart accessible design at Zappos. Getting to her current position of overseeing accessibility in design wasn't an easy path to take because it required a lot of time outside of her everyday job to build initial awareness around this initiative; however, her passion motivated her and she took every chance she could to bring awareness to accessibility.

"My determination for this initiative ultimately led me to become the go-to person for accessibility design within the organization," Allie said. "Once this became clear, I realized the opportunity for it to hold an official role within the company."

Allie's experience highlights the complexities of accessible design and the need for more people to be involved. However, Allie only really focused on accessibility—imagine what it would take to be truly inclusive?

In order for Allie to move into an official role with accessibility design, she needed to prove the need. She conducted a ton of research and created a presentation that laid out both the customer and financial benefits of this new role—including the reduced development costs of designing inclusively at the onset. Upon review, the company agreed to create the position for her.

Greg Williams, Accessibility Program Office Executive from Deque Systems, calculates costs related to accessibility in his article, "The Huge Cost of Ignoring Accessibility When Designing Your Website."[32]

In terms of lawsuits related to accessibility:

- "Using average compensation and labor timeframes gathered in the course of our work with Fortune 50 companies,

---

32   Greg Williams, "The huge cost of ignoring accessibility when designing your website," *The Next Web*, September 27, 2019.

we estimated that addressing…a single web accessibility complaint (a complaint through the ADA) costs almost $10,000."

- "A simple and quickly settled digital accessibility lawsuit would cost the defendant an estimated $350,000."

Another argument people bring up against designing inclusively is that there are not many out there who are in need of inclusive products; however, the disposable income of various communities show that this is not the case:

- Working-Age Americans with disabilities: $490 billion

- Black Americans: $501 billion

- Hispanic Americans: $582 billion

To sum it up, "People with disabilities represent 35 percent of working-age adults—that's twenty million people. If your website is not accessible, you are locking out huge market segments." [35]

Assumptions that businesses make when there is not user need for accessibility have made people hesitant to accept inclusive design. However, these numbers show there is not only huge cost associated with not being accessible, but a large revenue opportunity in being accessible and inclusive. To do this effectively? Be inclusive from the start.

"The fact that if you solve for accessibility up front, it alleviates time, money, resources, headache, all of that, you know, down the road," Allie explained. "I'm always on a broken record saying this needs to be addressed up front. The focus and time and resources need to be put into this, this chunk of work up front, to allow us to truly scale ourselves in the future and not have to constantly go back and fix things… that's very expensive."

CURRENT STATE OF DIGITAL ACCESSIBILITY

Allie's initiative to focus on accessibility is something we need to see reflected more throughout the internet. The analysis that WebAIM did on the top million home pages of websites exposes how inadequate accessibility of websites is. WebAIM "seeks multifaceted collaborations with organizations seeking to foster an internal culture of accessible design and development, holistically at all levels."[33] Upon analyzing the top websites, they found that "the rate of WCAG non-conformance and the number of errors present are slowly *increasing* over time."

Between their study done in 2019 and 2020, they saw a downward trend in conforming to WCAG (Web Content Accessibility Guidelines), which sets the guidelines of how to make websites accessible. In order to test the million website home pages, WebAIM used WAVE. "WAVE uses heuristics and logic to detect end-user accessibility barriers and Web Content Accessibility Guidelines (WCAG) conformance failures," but note that this engine only catches "25 percent to 35 percent of possible conformance failures." More errors can exist. [33]

---

33 "The WebAIM Million," *WebAIM.*

The study found that "across the one million home pages, 60,909,278 distinct accessibility errors were detected—an average of 60.9 errors per page" and the complexity of home pages also increased since more elements were being used. "Users with disabilities would expect to encounter detectable errors on one in every fourteen home page elements with which they engage."[33]

The top two issues WebAIM found were:

1. **Low Contrast Text.** Having low contrast text makes it difficult to read, and not only for people with visual impairments. Think of light blue text on a light grey background. This WCAG failure was present in 86.3 percent of the one million home pages.

2. **Missing Alternative Text.** Alt text adds a description to things that aren't text, like pictures or diagrams. How can a screen reader read an image without alt text? Screen readers are "technology [that] helps people who are blind or who have low vision to use information technology with the same level of independence and privacy as anyone else. Screen readers are also used by people with certain cognitive or learning disabilities, or users who simply prefer audio content over text."[34] But, when there is an image with no alt text, the screen reader will ignore it unless they changed the setting to reading off the file name.[37] This failure was present in 66 percent of analyzed websites.

---

34 "Designing for Screen Reader Compatibility," *WebAIM*.

The other issues WebAIM found were empty links (59.9 percent), missing form labels (53.8 percent), empty buttons (28.7 percent), and missing document language (28 percent)[33]. These errors were found in top, frequently used websites. It shows us that we have so much more work to do in accessibility to make sure people aren't constantly running into barriers when trying to use the things we create.

Another person I spoke with about business and inclusion was Danielle Oberst Salisbury, who I met during her visit to Seattle.

The Husky Union Building (HUB) at UW was loud and crowded at lunch time, with students rushing to get food between class or claiming study tables during their lunch break. When Danielle offered to commute to the U District and meet me in the HUB, I had no idea how we were going to find each other. After some texting back and forth, I told her what I was wearing, figuring that although it may not be a professional way to communicate, it could still be effective. I was still a college student, so I had a pass.

While preparing to talk to Danielle about her experience at Microsoft, I studied and admired her work history. Danielle's careers all lean toward management. She worked as a project manager at Insight International, UX manager at Microsoft, project manager at Zulily, and technical product manager at Zappos. Zappos, the company she is with now, caught my eye in particular. When I went on their LinkedIn page, their most recent post was about inclusion. After asking her about inclusive design at Zappos, we had a discussion about decision making and problem solving.

In a perfect world, things would be designed and based solely around user need; however, companies still need to make a profit. Navigating the balance of cost and benefit can be informed by research. One example is from Danielle's experience at Zulily, an online retailer, on whether or not they should create alt text, or descriptive captions, for the text on images of graphic T-shirts in their MVP (Minimal Viable Product) before launching.

"There's a cost associated with everything you do to make a code change," Danielle said. "It was really, really expensive to do this virtually because the site changes every day. So if somebody would have had to make a program to read all of this text...you'd have to do it for every single product."

After debating what to do, they decided to make the alt text for the graphic T-shirt images say there was text on the clothes for the MVP, "so it lets the person know that there's text on this and if they want to further research it they can do so using whatever methods that they want to, but we decided not to screen read everything on the graphic."

In coming to this conclusion, the team had tried screen readers themselves and tested their MVP with focus groups. What I like most about Zulily's approach is how informed their decision was, investigating the option of alt text for graphic T-shirts on their online store. During their investigation, they learned that making the images of graphic T shirts product alt text "ended up being actually a lot of cognitive load" for the user.

I found it interesting that their research took on the qualitative angle of cognitive load, which is the mass of information you are exposing the user to at once. If the cognitive load is too high, the user might be overwhelmed and have a negative experience, leading them to stop using the product. Knowing this, they decided not to pursue developing a way to create alt text for images at this time.

In addition to enhancing companies financially, these companies also need to be inclusive legally.

"There's different tiers of accessibility so you can be tier one approved or tier two. And each tier has different criteria. They're implementing it more and more, different companies are making it a requirement, the government's making a requirement for websites and apps to be ADA compliant, to have a certain tier of accessibility...A lot of companies are trying to do more and get to a higher tier."

There are two sides to setting legal requirements to be at a certain state of inclusion. On one side, making certain levels of accessibility a requirement will force companies to incorporate accessible design. On the other hand, companies may take these requirements and not try to make their products more inclusive beyond what the requirements state. Additionally, regardless of having laws that state creators will have to be inclusive, Joe Clark, who wrote *Building Accessible Websites*, calculated that "retrofitting always costs more," which is a compelling reason that for-profit companies should incorporate inclusion without making those standards compulsive.

Fortunately, a lot of the decisions in favor of accessibility are judgment calls made by the front-line designers, and Danielle explains that this makes it important for accessibility to be considered among user experience (UX) designers in addition to people in the legal system or engineering side of production.

"The rules only say so much, right?" Danielle said. "I think the best place for [accessibility] to live is user experience because that's really the right role and discipline to figure out how you make something compliant and user-friendly. An engineer can make something compliant all day long but it won't necessarily be the best user experience...or legal can come in and say 'we're applying all of these rules to all of these things' and then you have just a black and white website, you know, because that's technically compatible."

Right now, Zappos has one UX design team that other teams can use when they need to; however, Danielle makes sure to always have a UX designer on her personal team. The participation of somebody looking at user experience can ensure that design modifications to improve inclusion are not just the bare minimum change to meet a legal standard. People in UX are equipped with skills to incorporate user needs at all stages of design, and the more the diversity included, the more creative the designers get to be. Needing to be more creative for a wider user group can end up creating a product designed much better and more usable for many situations outside of the intended use case.

A large part of avoiding inclusive design is because businesses cannot see the financial benefit right away, despite an expanded customer base. Constraints that fuel creativity and improve the quality of the products will have financial benefits in the long run. This has to start during the design process in order to make it work, because going back to adapt a solution later will be more costly.

We have the power to design for some of these challenges. Designing solutions is going to be hard, but we didn't join the industry and receive opportunities to not create impact.

To scale up my own influence, I embarked on the journey of writing this book, not only to learn about inclusive design, but to share my findings so that others could also make an impact for inclusion in their work. It's not going to stop here. Something you read in this book is going to compel you to make an impact through your own inclusive mindset. What is it and how are you going to scale it?

LET'S INCLUSIFY

- Incorporating inclusive practice from the beginning removes the costs of having to go back and fix things to be compliant with accessibility regulations.

- Disregarding the practice of inclusion can result in expensive lawsuits, which can be raised by the ADA for inaccessibility.

- Practice defining accessibility constraints to force designers to be more creative, thereby making a better design for all users.

INCLUDING CULTURES

"Anyone can be made to feel like an outsider. It's up to the people who have the power to exclude."

—MELINDA GATES

Globalization. With quickly advancing technology, our world has achieved a state where people from all over the world can interact with each other in seconds. Companies leverage this ability to reach a larger audience for their products, which is known as globalization. A key factor in making globalization work is intentionally making the product or service appropriate for the other culture.

An example of when a company marketed wrongly was McDonald's. Most will have heard about the different meals offered in different countries. McDonald's has restaurants all over the world, in more than one hundred countries. Unfortunately, in marketing for the World Cup soccer championship in 1994, they printed flags of the competing nations and included the Saudi Arabia flag, which has a quote from the Qur'an, on their bags. By printing words from the Qur'an on the bag, which is meant for disposal, McDonald's offended Muslim communities.[35] [36]

McDonalds didn't do their culturalization homework. Culturalization means making sure content is appropriate for the culture it is being used within. This was designing exclusively because they did not consider how other cultures would be affected by the design that they created. Had they ensured it was appropriate to put national flags on items meant for disposal, they might have learned that it is disrespectful to put verses from the Qur'an in a position where they would be thrown away.

---

35 Associated Press, "Saudi Flags on Burger Bags: A Big MacStake: Marketing: Muslims complained that McDonald's World Cup packaging sent Koran verse to the trash bin," *Los Angeles Times,* June 8, 1994.

36 Dirk Beveridge, "McDonald's Backs Off Promotion That Offended Muslims; Coca-Cola Draws Fire." *AP News,* June 8, 1994.

CONSEQUENCE OF CULTURALIZATION IN VIDEO GAMES

Another example of the importance of this phenomenon can be seen in the product that 2.5 billion people around the world use: video games. It is projected these gamers will collectively spend $196 billion dollars in 2022 on gaming products.[37]

With this quickly growing industry (which has extended into the global market), making the content appropriate for the global audience is a crucial aspect of making money in this industry.

Kate Edwards explained to me the importance of culturalization work for globalization. She is currently the Executive Director of the Global Game Jam and CEO of Geogrify (a company that provides consultation on culturalization) and was previously Executive Director of the International Game Developers Association. Her extensive experience highlights how crucial culturalization is in inclusive considerations.

"It's basically the idea that we need to check certain content, the certain form of content risk which is all of the more qualitative geopolitical and cultural factors," Kate said. "What are those factors that influence the perception of content, the creation of content, and dealing with the biases of the content creators?"

Biases are hugely impactful in creating content. Unconscious biases are more dangerous since they lead to assumptions

---

37 Tom Wijman, "The Global Games Market Will Generate $152.1 Billion in 2019 as the US Overtakes China as the Biggest Market," *New Zoo*, June 18, 2019.

that inform the design decisions instead of data informing the design decisions.

> *"Unconscious bias is part of social and evolutionary programming. Culture, family, and personal experience hardwire human brains to make unconscious decisions. Biases help us navigate the world without being overwhelmed by information. Unconsciously our brains cluster people into groups based on traits to help make sense of our surroundings. The downside is that the potential for prejudice is hard-wired into human cognition. These unconscious biases skew how we perceive the world...When unconscious bias seeps into product design, it can lead to serious consequences."*[38]

These consequences can include disrespecting a religion or a culture. Creating something from assumptions causes a weak foundation for the design. Kate explains that a factor in culturalization work is for the content creators to understand that they do have biases, because everybody has biases, and they need to examine them.

"It's just realistic if you're a human being, you're biased," Kate said. "So, it's basically on the creation side—what are the factors on the creation side that are affecting the content creation? These stereotypes...oftentimes are related to a bias, but sometimes you're dealing with good intentioned people who just don't know...because they're not from that cultural group."

---

38   K.T. Lynn, "Design Matters: Engineering Design is Facing an Unconscious Bias Problem," *The Warren Centre*, May 17, 2019.

In the course of her consulting work, Kate must consider two different ways that the content of the games will be viewed in terms of culturalization:

1. The street level → How would a consumer react?

2. The political level → How would the government react?

Kate explained that "One is reacting from a consumer standpoint, so that's kind of the person on the street, how would they react to this. And then another level is the political level, so how will the government react to this."

Despite what creators' personal beliefs are, when they are creating content for someone else, advocating for those beliefs can cause problems. While Kate was at Microsoft, there was somebody who called Taiwan the Republic of China in a product by Microsoft. This example brings to light how impactful culturalization is in terms of politics.

"He's [the content creator] married to someone from Taiwan, and he's very much pro-independence for Taiwan, anti-China, and he just decided to do this as his way of expressing that political opinion. And that's not the place to do it. It's not your product...it's Microsoft's product...so his action got Microsoft in trouble in China...the head of Microsoft China, the subsidiary, was taken away for questioning for two days for subversion of the state."

The political considerations of culturalization are different in the US than they are in other countries, where there is more government control of content distribution. In the US, retailers control what they distribute in their businesses. Large companies like Target and Walmart have decency standards and are more family oriented. "If you look at it from that perspective...would Walmart ever stock porn in their video section, or would Target? No, that's never going to happen," Kate said. "This is why most games are not classified as 'adult only' (not including games seventeen or eighteen plus), due to the culture of the companies. Retailers won't stock them."

This example brings up a topic about identity/beliefs and culture. When are times we should advocate our beliefs, and when should we not? This is a complex topic, but fundamentally we need to be aware of our position on who we are representing at the time, and what our position is in the culture we are becoming involved in. In my experience, clothing choice while studying abroad has come up from professors before going to parts of South Africa and India, where it is culturally normal/acceptable to be dressed more conservatively than we might be used to in hotter climates. A question to think about is, what are we studying abroad for? To learn about a new culture, or to make this culture learn about ours? Regardless of whether we intend to be advocating a certain belief system with our actions, we need to consider how it is seen from other people's perspectives.

LOGICAL CONSISTENCY

People generally think of inclusion and diversity as a positive thing; however, Kate has seen that people can get upset about the push toward diversity in gaming environments.

"It's not necessarily a pushback against inclusion itself," Kate said. "To me it's a cultural difference, what they don't like is the concept that their games are going to be altered just for the sake of inclusivity."

When it comes to culturalization, Kate explained that there is "logical consistency" behind design decision in the games. "Every game, just like every film and TV show and everything else, is a world that gets created for a narrative purpose. And so, there will be times where you create a world but maybe it makes sense to have everyone on the planet be white, or Asian, or black, or whatever they might be. If there's logic to the narrative behind it—what I would call logical consistency—that's fine."

There is still a push back if people feel like the logic behind things are wrong, like the example Kate shared below.

"[When] Battlefield Five came out, they showed that there was a woman on the cover of the game taking place in World War II. And so a vocal minority were saying, *'That doesn't make any sense that there were women fighting World War II. Why are you showing a woman fighting in this, why do you need to have a woman fighting?'* you know, and it was mostly men [saying this]. It's like well, first of all, it's not true. Certainly, there were women who fought...they weren't drafted into the army because that didn't happen back then, but there were certainly many examples of women who fought during World War II, where they basically picked up arms and just did it themselves. So, there is historical precedent for it so it's not necessarily inaccurate. But...some of these people are just like *'We feel it's inaccurate and therefore it messes up the game.'*"

It is interesting to point out that in Kate's example, she said, "We [the vocal minority] feel like it's inaccurate." These people are going off what they "feel" is right, and not what was actually the historical fact. This feeling was based off an assumption which shows how critical it is to examine the assumptions you do have about certain things. Similar to how content creators need to check their biases, everyone (even the consumers) can think about how they are thinking and then see if their emotions are based on something they assumed, or something that actually happened.

Often times, I find myself upset over an aspect of a design, thinking about precedence or what would happen if that particular feature did not exist. This applies to more than design. When studying abroad in South Africa, our program hired a cook for when we were in the more rural parts of the Eastern Cape. She kept cooking lasagna, and at first we thought it was because we were Westerners and wondered if that's what she thought we typically ate. After thinking more about it, I realized it was probably easier to put together and bake a lasagna than to cook anything else, considering that we were a group of about thirty college students.

Another example of logical consistency can be how it is the reason for the lack of diversity in a video game. Kate told me about a game that demonstrates this:

"One hundred years from now, let's say the Japanese were successful in launching the colony ship to another planet. All staff, the Japanese astronauts, and people, they all go to this planet to create a new civilization. Well that planet is going to be pretty much all Japanese. And, you know, that's the way it's going to be...Is that racist, lacking diversity? Well no, there's a logical reason for it, the history of the planet is that it was created by a Japanese colony mission, and it's completely understandable. And it's completely defensible."

There should always be a reason behind each design decision. Question decisions. If there is a logical answer, then of course design it like that. If not, consider if it can be replaced with a more logical design.

Disregarding logical consistency, people might be unhappy about the diversity in their video games because they feel like an agenda is being pushed on them.

Kate further explained, "They don't like the idea that there are what they would call 'social justice warriors,' like myself, people who have the mission of diversity....They don't like that this is forced upon them....That's really what they're fighting against, it's the pushing of an agenda."

This "vocal minority" Kate talked about really is the minority in terms of consumers; in this case, the people who protest having their games "altered for inclusion."

"We already know that game players are diverse, they are very diverse," Kate said. "People who play games come from pretty much every demographic background you can imagine, age-wise, ethnicity-wise, religion-wise, geography, culture. Games are becoming a ubiquitous form of entertainment. If we already have all these people playing games from very diverse backgrounds, to me we should be making content that is represented with people who are already playing games."

Even with people like Kate who are making sure that games are following a logical consistency based on the type of culture in which they are based, games are still excluding certain communities. A big reason for this is since content creators wouldn't always know about different user perspectives, they are worried about getting something wrong and dealing with the backlash of not being politically correct.

SCARED OF DOING IT WRONG?

"If you ask any of these developers, no matter what their background is, they will tell you, *'I would love it for anyone to play the game. I don't want only certain people playing my game—I want everyone to enjoy what I've created.'* And I think that's pretty much true of every single creative person in any creative field is that, at some level deep down, they would love to have their work enjoyed by as many people as possible." explains Kate.

Here Kate explains more bluntly that the people creating games are not trying to be exclusive. Why create a game where typically the goal is for it to be used for entertainment, for only a small percentage of the population? A reason games might be exclusive is that the content creators either do not realize they weren't inclusive, or they weren't confident with creating something with inclusion for populations that they are not familiar with.

Kate said that, "If you try and represent a certain cultural background or ethnic background without having someone from that background or actually being the one creating it, you will be challenged very quickly by people and called out in a very negative way."

This is a big issue for companies to deal with, not to mention how the designer would feel about their mistake. To avoid this, people omit diverse representation from the game, even though including it means so much to the people playing the game that the income will pay off on the extra time and money it might take to design inclusively.

One way to make sure the designs are going to be correctly inclusive is by including people from the diverse groups we are trying to incorporate into the design process. For example, the game *Never Alone* included a main character from an indigenous group from Northern Canada. *Never Alone* was done well because the content creators went to the indigenous people to ask them and design along them to ensure everything was accurate.[39]

This is similar to incorporating users early in the design process within the UX industry. By going back to the user and understanding the context within which they are using the service or product, the finished outcome will be highly effective.

An example of this success is the adaptive controller Microsoft designed and then shared with other companies to make gaming inclusive for people with physical disabilities.

In order to create this success, Kate highlighted that, "They didn't guess. I mean, that controller was based on input from hundreds and hundreds of people with physical disability.

---

39 Kate Edwards, "Indigenous issues," *MultiLingual*, September 2014, page 20.

They asked them directly, '*What do you need from us, what can we make that's going to be universal enough to, you know, apply and be used for a lot of different situations?*' because a lot of people are unique in their disability."

Microsoft collaborated with many other parties, including a group called Able Gamers, a nonprofit that focuses on gamers with physical disabilities. After developing this product, they shared the design with companies like Sony and Nintendo to expand the inclusion of the gaming world to a larger audience. What made this controller so effective for its users was the fact that the users were involved in the first place.

In this chapter, you can see how impactful including cultures can be, on both the intended cultures and cultures that still use the product. It is a sad and exclusive society that gets upset over this push for inclusion; however, it is my hope inclusion will rise to a priority in terms of awareness for companies with both local and global reach. Even the act of seeing other cultures being included fills me with hope that the world is taking down one exclusive wall at a time. We still have a ways to go in both fighting for inclusion and against the people who believe incorporating diverse cultures and people is a negative change. We are stripping them of their typical comfort, broadening their perspectives, and adding interest and beauty in their daily lives.

LET'S INCLUSIFY

- There's going to be more than one affected stakeholder for your designs. Practice identifying them and ask yourself: how are their cultural values different from yours?

- Practice narrating the logical consistency of your story to ensure that the decisions make sense.

- Be proactive about what you don't know and learn more by designing with the user.

INNOVATING FOR INCLUSION

"What we really need to do to design is look at the extremes. The weakest, the person with arthritis, the athlete, the strongest, fastest person. Because when we understand what the extremes are, the middle will take care of itself."

—OBJECTIFIED[40]

---

40 *Objectified*, directed by Gary Hustwit (2009; Plexi Productions), Documentary.

There are many failed innovations that people didn't really know about, such as Cheetos Lip Balm and Watermelon Oreos. There are others that people *did* know about but didn't care enough to make them become successful, like Google+ (sorry Google). But what about the failures to be inclusive in millions of designs we use every day? You need two hands to play with a game controller, enough strength to pull down on the toilet handle, and the ability to step up on stairs.

The simplest definition of innovation comes from Merriam-Webster: "1) a new idea, method, or device, 2) the introduction of something new."[41] Innovation is what people strive for in the world of creation: innovative products, innovative systems, and innovative ways to experience things. There are innovations in home cleaning products (cordless vacuums), transportation (Uber), and technology (any of the devices that you use). A lot of these innovations have been focused in tangible products, and this might be because of how the tech industry exploded in this century. Innovation is now a buzzword and necessity in all things.

The upside of this exploding economy is all the conveniences and solved problems it has brought to some of us; however, a good point Heath Sadlier made in a *Medium* blog is that "the obsession with building things quickly can lead to a confused approach, a confused idea of what success looks like, or even to ensure the right things are being measured."[42]

---

41   "Definition of Innovation," Merriam-Webster.

42   Heath Sadlier, "Tackling Assumption Monsters by Embracing Ambiguity and Curiosity," *Medium,* May 27, 2017.

One example of something that wasn't mentioned in the success of a lot of products was inclusion. After these advances in technology, it's time to start innovating the process to make things more inclusive to the intended user, as opposed to what Sadlier describes as the HIPPO: Highest Paid Person's Opinion.[42] This person only has one perspective from one life experience, so how is it they are allowed to control the design process?

Claire Lorman, in her *Medium* blog "Practicing What We Preach on Inclusivity," stated: "For too long, products and services have lacked the most basic element of inclusivity— actually including the beneficiaries of the end result in the design process from the very beginning."[43]

In order to truly innovate the design process to incorporate inclusion, which is a crucial aspect to incorporate moving forward in the design and creation world, we need to innovate the design process.

This can look like including diverse users in the design processes. This does not mean to start doing participatory design and using those designs as your own; instead, participatory design can show you what features are the most important to that user and take those understandings to incorporate into your own. Other ways to include a diverse array of users in the design processes is doing research with them so you understand the environment in which your designs will be utilized.

---

43 Claire Lorman, "Practicing What We Preach on Inclusivity," *Medium*, December 16, 2018.

Doing research on your users helps identify the constraints that you have to design within to make sure your idea is inclusive. The process in the story I learned about from an interview with Samuel Rajkumar, CEO of Heuristic Devices and co-founder of the Foundation for Environmental Monitoring (FFEM), follows these main steps:

1. Identify Constraints

2. Work with the Experts

3. Iterate on Prototypes

INNOVATION FROM CONSTRAINTS

In the first month of studying abroad in India, I had the opportunity to meet with Sam. I was interested in talking to him because of his work innovating the way people can test water and soil to make the testing process more accessible to farmers and rural villages that would benefit most from this technology. Testing in laboratories is not only expensive, but physically inaccessible to those who need to get prompt results.

Learning about Sam's process through innovating the technology of water and soil testing provided a perfect case study. I was able to break down his process into the three steps laid out in the previous section.

IDENTIFY CONSTRAINTS

Problems people face in terms of testing water or soil are:

- **Cost of laboratory testing.** It costs hundreds of rupees to get a water sample tested at a lab.

- **Ability to go to the laboratory.** It is hard to get the water sample to a laboratory, especially for rural villagers.

"A laboratory is 100 km away, and nobody is going to take that water voluntarily 100 km away. Nobody is going to do that," according to Sam.

These two constraints made it difficult for people to test their water, which creates a huge problem because of the prevalence of unsafe water in India. "If we have ten hand pumps in a village, maybe three are safe and seven are unsafe, but we have no way of knowing. There's no taste. The only way to know is to test."

In order to solve this problem, the FFEM made a field kit that that costs only twenty rupees per test, as opposed to the few hundreds it would cost at a lab. It is also extremely accurate. "We did hundreds of tests and had a correlation of 0.997...almost indistinguishable from a laboratory test" (Note: FFEM still emphasizes to the users that they should eventually get the water tested at a lab).

They have also solved the problem of access to laboratories by making it possible to use a smart phone to test the sample onsite. After a while, FFEM expanded their testing to include soil so farmers could see what type of fertilizer they would need for each crop, or if the soil was even right for the crop they wanted to plant.

WORK WITH EXPERTS

What would be the use of traveling all the way to a farm or a rural village, just to point out their issues and leave? FFEM needed to bring a solution with them.

"We don't go in alone to a rural area and say test your soil or whatever you want to do," Sam explained. "We go with partners who go '*Oh, you got this? Well here's fertilizer, or here's inexpensive other fertilizer,*' and so on."

Since FFEM understands that different regions face unique problems they wouldn't understand completely, they make sure to go with partners who know the area. This way they are providing solutions that match both the needs of the people and will work well with the environment.

Sam told me that "these farmers and these local organizations are working with villagers. They know, they say, for example, '*Hey, this guy can't afford the fertilizer recommendation so why don't we use one he can [afford].*' They know the situation better than we can even imagine."

FFEM included guides familiar with local conditions of the stakeholder community. The guide provided a level of communication that let them deliver solutions inclusively to match specific stakeholder needs.

ITERATE ON PROTOTYPES

The design they have now is inclusive in terms of affordability and accessibility, and they are developing the training aspect of the solution to be inclusive. Although people can be trained to test the samples, it is not 100 percent intuitive enough for somebody to pick up and use.

"It's very easy to do," Sam said. "If I train you for an hour, anybody should be able to do it. Even somebody who is semi-literate. But that is something that we cannot scale. I cannot have a low-cost kit that has training, so that is what we are struggling with right now. We have a couple of prototypes in the works that should cut down even that."

By continuously iterating on something that does work for the initial constraints, FFEM is innovating in a different space to design a more inclusive way to test water and soil. They are constantly asking, "How do we make it cheaper, how do we make it better, how do we add value to a farmer or for a rural villager?"

By forcing themselves to become more inclusive, they are becoming innovators at the forefront of this design space in a way that no other organization has been able to do (proving the statistic that inclusive companies are more likely to be leaders of innovation in that industry from the introduction).[44] Creating inside their constraints, relying on people who truly understand the unique conditions faced by individual stakeholders, and iterating on what they have makes them inclusive innovators.

Doing all of this is hard work. It was accomplished through hundreds of tests and many prototypes. Even though I broke

---

44 "6 Statistics That Will Convince You to Prioritize Diversity & Inclusion," Teamable Blog, Teamable.

down FFEM's process into three steps, there was still so much work done to accomplish what they have so far, and a lot of work ahead to continue toward new accomplishments. Do not take these steps as the only things that make something innovative; innovation doesn't come through the use of shiny new tools or fancy vocabulary, which, if overused, makes their meaning lose value. It comes through iterating in constrained design spaces where we are forced to be creative.

A dangerous part of innovation in design projects, however, is thinking you are being innovative because of the language people are using when designing.

BEWARE OF THE BUZZ

A simple personal example: I don't like drawings of butter-flies. I like pictures of them, and I like watching them flutter around amongst flowers, but I would never buy anything that has a drawing of a butterfly on it. Seeing them drives me crazy. After thinking more about why this was the case, I realized it was because I felt like throughout my life, I saw cartoon butterflies everywhere: in books, on TV, etc. Their popularity made them lose value, especially since the cartoon drawings were never actually that representative of their delicate beauty.

This case can also be applied to the words created to make targeted impacts in the design world, but an example from Erika Bailey on Medium shows otherwise:

"It's exciting at first, and then the inevitable crash happens where people say, for example, 'Design Thinking. That's *so last year' or, 'Design Thinking? I did that two years ago. Didn't work.'*[45]

Innovation is going to change the world of inclusion, but in order for it to make an impact, we need to start implementing different ways of designing in a way that will move beyond talking like innovative designers, to creating like innovative designers.

LET'S INCLUSIFY

- Innovation is achieved through the practice of innovative processes.

- Keep iterating after working through initial constraints.

- Beware of the value of words we use. What are some words you use now, and which have lost their value in your work and practices?

---

45 Erika Bailey, "Beyond Buzzword: Innovation and Design Thinking," *Medium*, August 20, 2019.

INTERSECTIONALITY
OF INCLUSION

---

*"What if designers were more inclusive in their process and
shared more skillsets in order to strengthen the final output
by working through the design solutions better?"*

—HALLE KHO[46]

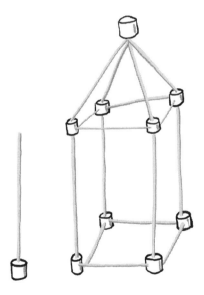

---

46   Halle Kho, "Taking Risks Inside the Design Process," *frog* (blog).

How many identities do you have?

The one that most people might associate you with is the race they assume you are, but you're part of many other identity groups: your gender, family traditions, and social life. Do you spend your weekends at the club or chilling with Netflix? Are you liberal or conservative?

People can identify themselves in many ways. What we build into our own culture of identities (or what identities others might impose on us) creates a web of intersections. For some, these intersections can be the compounded disparities of exclusion or the privledge that contribute to inclusion.

The realm of inclusion is large and diverse and intersectional. Aspects of inclusion can be matched differently to encompass more use cases and create a better experience for everyone involved.

For example, Beth Kolko from the University of Washington created a device for a community with limited resources in Africa, which is now being utilized within larger hospitals in the US because it is easier to use. I heard her talk about the story of DripAssist in an Intro to Human Centered Design and Engineering class as an example of something created so well (after multiple iterations, of course) to the point where many other people could adopt it. On the ShiftLabs website, it explains that DripAssist can "manage and monitor IV drips easily without pumps and confidently use gravity infusion. No need for asset tracking, calibration, or maintenance."[47]

---

47   "DRIP ASSIST," DripAssist Human, Shift Labs.

Beth Kolko wanted to create something that would help nurses in resource-limited communities accurately set the IV drips so patients would be receiving the correct amount of medicine. Previously they would have to spend time doing the math for the rate of IV fluid in their head and time it on their watches, which left a lot of room for human error. Where the US had large expensive machines, these nurses in a small African community could only rely on their own mental math and multitasking. After researching and pro-totyping, DripAssist was born, which solved the problems the nurses had; however, because of how well it was designed, Doctors Without Borders also began using the device, as well as larger US hospitals.

DripAssist was successful because the design of this handheld tool satisfied needs in the intersections between cost and convenience. Meeting multiple intersections of need is what makes products inclusive. As we realize all of the identities we have, or cultures we are part of, we can acknowledge how each one has either a benefit or a need according to the way that society has been designed. By designing for these different needs, we can be more inclusive.

Another intersection we can create for is between design and different software platforms; an idea introduced to me by Danielle.

I was originally interested in talking to Danielle because she was one of the people involved in designing emojis for Micro-soft. When designing emojis, several factors need to be consid-ered: skin tone, cultures, and even the way the emojis are facing each other. However, before digging into this, Danielle started out explaining an inclusive design factor I had never thought of—inclusion between how devices interact with each other.

EMOJI COMPATIBILITY BETWEEN DEVICES

Do you remember when you would receive a text, and in the message a small black outline of a rectangle [] would appear? At first you ignored it, because you didn't know what it was, but then as it kept happening, you wondered what you were missing out on. Or maybe you were the one sending the text message with your specifically chosen emoji, and you didn't get the response you thought you would. This happened all the time when I was in high school, and it drove me crazy! At some point I learned it was because the people texting me had iPhones, and I had an Android sliding phone, but the specifics were lost to me. I didn't realize how different the platforms were, much less that Android and iOS both existed and were different from each other.

This problem must have happened to everyone who was sending each other emojis, right?

Wrong. Maybe this was the case in the United States, but not internationally.

"This was right when the emojis were pretty popular on Google and Apple, and of course they were in Japan on all three of their carriers." Danielle explained. "They have three main carriers in Japan for their cell phone companies and all of them are compatible with each other. Okay, so they're leading the way in emojis. They introduced scanner compatibility as their design goal. So, we thought what if we did that at Microsoft, had all of our emojis be compatible with all of our platforms, the operating system, the cloud services, and the mobile system. And then we thought, 'Well, what if we made them compatible with Unicode, so they could show up on other people's devices too?' because at that time, an emoji that wasn't compatible with a device would show you a square box."

Danielle and her team worked through this problem of compatibility by using Unicode. Unicode's website explains what Unicode is and why it is important:[48]

"Before Unicode was invented, there were hundreds of different systems, called character encodings, for assigning these numbers. These early character encodings were limited and could not contain enough characters to cover all the world's languages....The Unicode Standard provides a unique number for every character, no matter what platform, device, application or language. It has been adopted by all modern software providers and now allows data to be transported through many different platforms, devices, and applications."

Emojis are revolutionizing texting. In fact, "over nine hundred million emojis are sent every day without text" and "there are more than 2,800 emojis and most of them (nearly 2,300) are used each and every day."[49] Making them compatible is important because the incompatibilities exclude people from sharing these tiny images that have been incorporated into our language, with impacts that can change the whole meaning of a sentence and contribute to self-expression of emotions.

---

48 "What is Unicode?" General Information, Unicode.

49 Jeremy Burge, "Facebook Reveals Most and Least Used Emojis," *Emojipedia*, July 13, 2018.

In a BBC Future article, Neil Cohn explains how emojis are augmenting our language through texting:[50]

"When emojis appear with text, they often supplement or enhance the writing. This is similar to gestures that appear along with speech. Over the past three decades, research has shown that our hands provide important information that often transcends and clarifies the message in speech. Emoji serve this function too—for instance, adding a kissy or winking face can disambiguate whether a statement is flirtatiously teasing or just plain mean."

Emojis have become an important communication medium for online communication; people even use them in emails! There are two different types of intersections present in the use of emojis: one being technology and design, which is solved by mapping them to Unicode, and the other being culture and globalization, because of the global reach of these tiny pictures. Both needed to be considered and implemented in order to make them an inclusive emerging component of how people use language.

INTERSECTION OF TECHNOLOGICAL ACCESS AND CULTURE

In addition to providing unique encoding to characters, Unicode has standards that drove inclusivity in emoji design with Danielle's team.

---

50 Neil Cohn, "Will emoji become a new language?" *BBC Future*, October 13, 2015.

Danielle explained, "We wanted to be the most inclusive that we could be, and it was really serious for us because we were compliant to Unicode standards."

This was several years ago, when inclusive design was not implemented in common practice (not that it is now to the extent it should be). The designers needed to be very careful about their designs and intentional about what they would add or omit to the designs. The debate for the skin tone of people emojis was one problem they solved by looking at previous examples.

"We took a whole bunch of different people emojis that have been created in the past from different companies, and we took color droppers from Photoshop basically [to] find out what the hex value was." Danielle said. After taking the hex values, they chose the average hex code color to be the skin tone.

You might be wondering, why can't there just be several options of color for the same emoji? We have that now, but the technology for the ability to pick different versions of the same emoji was not available at the time Danielle and her team were making them, so they had to be really aware of what would make the designs inclusive. The technological constraints they faced pressured them into being creative with their decision-making process.

For other emojis, like the poop emoji, they based their decisions on the Unicode standards. Danielle explains that because they wanted to make the emojis as inclusive as possible for an international audience, they did not want to take creative liberties.

"We wanted to be the most inclusive we could be, and it was really serious for us because we were compliant to Unicode standards....We wanted to be very true to the Unicode definitions of different things. So we didn't want to take any liberties, any creative liberties really with anything that was defined. That's actually the reason why we did not have the face on the poop emoji....It doesn't say anything about [a] face in the Unicode definition. And so, we did a lot of research into Japanese culture, and there's this notion of the smiling happy poo. And it means good luck. The Unicode definition said nothing about this emoji being correlated with that concept so we were very careful to design it strictly according to Unicode standards without editorializing it."

Here are more considerations in creating emojis for an international audience, to show you the complexities of designing for the world and the massive amount of research that is needed:

"There was accessibility," Danielle explained. "There was ethnicity, race, skin tone. We also were mindful of LTR countries. So, any country that has a language that reads left to right (LTR). We could calculate the standard of which way all the vehicles are facing. So if they are facing forward, we may continue to make them forward, which is a lot of research into what different languages do and how different cultures use emojis. And we found out some interesting things, like it's actually very offensive if you put certain emojis in front of other emojis, especially with animals. So we made sure that all the animals are facing a specific way."

This mindset, which was common throughout web design, is being developed further today. In web accessibility textbooks

I read, most of them started with this misconception of how designing for accessibility, or, more broadly, inclusion, means that designers cannot be creative with their work. However, this mindset is changing as technology advances. Designs can be both beautiful and inclusive.

These emojis were manually checked to make sure they would not be offensive. Danielle explained, "They all got examined by different engineers from across the company, basically, and before you do a release at Microsoft, and pretty much anywhere before continuous deployment was a thing, every piece of code got triaged. And it came to this engineering board for review and luckily we had people who were from different cultures that called things out (such as the animal emojis facing the wrong way) and we were like, '*Okay, then we need to go back and relook at this.*' We worked closely with one of the design teams that Microsoft has in Japan... to incorporate their feedback."

The inclusive design of emojis is still being emulated. In an article from the *Washington Post* published in July 2019, Marie C. Baca explains Ryan McDearmont's criticism of a falafel plate emoji.[51] "Ryan McDearmont, an Austin-based social media manager who co-hosts a podcast on emoji aesthetics, said the most controversial addition among consumers may be not be one aimed at righting emoji's long history of homogeneity, but rather one that is meant to depict a plate of falafel. With both the Apple and Google versions of the falafel emoji, McDearmont said, 'it looks like a good emoji at

---

51   Marie C. Baca, "Why Emoji Are—Finally—Becoming More Diverse," *The Washington Post*, July 17, 2019.

a large size, but when it's smaller it looks like spaghetti and meatballs.' Others have compared the falafel emoji to a plate of rocks, potatoes, coconuts, or worse.'"[51]

People may think this is a small issue, but considering that there was a controversy about cheese being under the patty instead of above the patty in a hamburger emoji in the United States, we needed to make falafel more recognizable.

By expanding to a more inclusive mindset, we can have these "wins" of being inclusive on a way bigger scale. We can do this by developing our own inclusive mind and by talking to others to spread the word.

THE INCLUSIVE MIND

During a UX career fair, I spoke to a recruiter about how I was starting to write a book on inclusive design. He immediately brought up that someone at the tech company he worked at was kickstarting inclusive design within the company and suggested I reach out to her.

Annika is part of the customer operations team, where they focus on supporting their users and ensuring they get the best experience with the company's products. On top of this, Annika is also involved in both making parts of the program more accessible (like making sure components are still accessible after translating them into different languages) and working to improve the inclusive environment within the company.

"I've been really interested in making the product something that anyone and everyone can use," Annika explained. "So

I have kind of done various things here and there to try and gain awareness internally about matters of inclusivity and accessibility...awareness-building has been at the center of the work I've been doing."

When using the design program, Annika wanted to make sure that "anyone and everyone can have the same experience and everyone can get what they want out of [the product]." This interest in improving accessibility so everyone can participate in using the company's product made her look at the bigger picture, which is: how can she raise awareness about accessibility so more people will start to implement it in their work? Annika pinpointed what she needs to do to have a bigger impact on making the company's products more accessible, which is to cultivate an inclusive mindset.

"I recognize the biggest need is of awareness and a mindset shift, and I think this goes beyond any specific company, but just in general for society," Annika said. "In order to create something that everyone can use, we really need to get outside of our own heads."

To make the work of the company more inclusive, Annika was not only checking the accessibility of different features of the product, but also working to make a change in the mindset creators have about inclusion through conversations and sharing experiences. This is why we need to share the message about inclusive design, and it is something that we need to see implemented more through the culture of creating.

Being more inclusive overall through this mixing and matching of intersections leads to really cool solutions in all different types of products, whether they be physical or digital. By practicing how to develop an inclusive mind in examining these intersections of pain points, people can design more inclusively. This strategy may be hard to implement but will result in creative and usable solutions, from correct dosages of medicine to online communications.

LET'S INCLUSIFY

- Identify diversity at the intersections of race, equity, ability, and many more factors.

- Practice working your inclusive mind to influence others to do the same.

PART 3

INCLUSIFY YOUR MIND

This section discusses three concepts that can be examined and implemented for a more inclusive mindset: assumptions, normal, and empathy. Each chapter explores what these concepts are used for and how to employ them effectively. Throughout the chapters, reflect on your own experiences with these concepts.

EFFECTIVE-IZING
ASSUMPTIONS

"Industry archetypes are the enemy of inclusion."

—HUDSON TAYLOR[52]

---

52 Hudson Taylor, "Activating Change Through Allyship," *Journal of Intercollegiate Sport* 8, no. 1 (2015): 37-42.

Rolling hills covered in yellow straw-like grass were dotted with mud huts and grazing farm animals. This image sets the scene for my memory of the Eastern Cape in South Africa. During this study abroad program where we were learning about disability in communities with limited resources, we visited a home for children with disabilities. This "home" was a collection of mud huts with a plentiful garden that helped sustain them financially. The first day we went to visit, we walked around in these huts, which provided a surprisingly cool respite from the warm sun in the winter months of this region.

One of the huts, the largest one, was empty. It was painted spring green inside, and a bench was built into the wall, encircling most of it. Two long wooden tables were in the middle. The next hut was smaller and had a side room. It was dark; the windows didn't let in much light. Once my eyes adjusted, I could see a boy kneeling behind wooden posts that surrounded a small mattress, like a baby crib; but this boy wasn't a baby, he was maybe four or five years old. He stuck his arms out between the posts, holding the hands of my classmates who went up to say hello.

Later when we were heading back to the Donald Woods Center, the conversations started.

"Did you see that boy in the cage?"

"I can't believe they keep him in there."

"How can they force him to sit in that crib all day?"

The classmates were really concerned about this boy. They thought the caregivers left him in his bed all day and shared their concerns with our instructors.

The next day we visited this home, however, he was outside interacting with us. He came up to me, walking on his knees, the sloping ground made it too difficult for him to use his wheelchair, and grabbed my hand, leading me into the largest hut, chatting in Xhosa (the X sound is a click). Two adults were in the hut, and they laughed at what the boy was saying. Feeling awkward, I smiled and left to join the rest of the students.

We learned later that the reason this boy was in his bed when we had visited the day before was because it was during the children's naptime. This boy had bars around his bed because he often had seizures, so it was to protect him and make sure he didn't fall and hurt himself during an episode.

The assumptions my classmates had made created these negative feelings toward the organization, believing the boy was neglected and left in the bed all day; however, the reality was very different. Caregivers and other children walk around with him during the day, and on school days, one of the people working in the home takes him along with the other children to the local school to teach English.

In this example, students started devaluing the work of the home for children with disabilities because of what they thought about the boy's treatment. That whole evening students were talking about it and feeling upset. Their assumptions led them to the judgement that the home for children with disabilities was a bad place, when really it was the opposite.

Assumptions affect more than just social spaces and how people think of each other—they also have a big impact on creating experiences for others.

ASSUMPTION IN DESIGN

When makers use their assumptions to create things, whether they are projects, programs, or experiences, it contributes to exclusion in design. Designing with assumptions might look something like this:

1. Maker has assumption about the user from their own personal experiences related to the user

2. Maker develops user needs based off assumptions

3. The developed user needs inform design decisions

4. The final product solves the defined user needs

Put together, this is what it looks like:

Assumption + some research → user needs → design decisions → final product

Note that the user needs, which were informed by assumptions, directly affects what the final product becomes. We end up with a product whose foundation is tainted with assumptions, making it an unstable solution that will exclude people.

The assumption-informed design creating exclusion is what made my mom realize for the first time that she had a disability, and the implications of what that meant in terms of exclusion.

Assumptions about what a person can or cannot do leads to missed experiences and other people dictating what their abilities are. My mom, the hardest working person I have ever met, grew up in South Korea and got polio when she was three years old, then immigrated to the United States in her twenties. She shared her story of how assumptions of her ability led to her missed experiences of PE (Physical Education) and ultimately made her realize what the implications of having a disability meant in society.

When I asked her what it was like to grow up as a child with a disability, she told me that "until I go to the elementary school I don't even know I am disabled." She was so excited to go to school for the first time. "I still remember that teacher's name. I don't remember anybody's name, but my first grade teacher's name is Mrs. Ha."

"I had a great time, because I'm always a hyper person, happy," my mom said. "And I'm very confident with what I am learning over there. But we have a PE class. Even though I have polio, I'm just a little limping while walking around, and I want to go...and teacher said 'No, you cannot go, you cannot come out and do PE.'"

Instead of going to PE, Mrs. Ha told her she had to stay in the classroom as a "classroom keeper." Mrs. Ha told her, "Chin, it's your job to watch when everybody is not there," but she didn't like it. When the other kids came back from PE, they wondered why she wasn't there too.

My mom explained that, "Some kid said, '*Oh, I wish I can stay with you, I hate PE,*' and, '*How come you didn't go out there,*' some people complaining. And some people, you know, they say, because I'm different than other people, that's why I stay there? So that's the start, after PE, my first PE, then I start to realize that I'm not like other people. Other people can do—I cannot do that."

This story of my mom's experience can also be applied to how assumptions dictated her experiences:

1. Teacher has an assumption about my mom's abilities based on how she walks.

2. The "need" that the teacher identified was that my mom could not partake in physical activities because of the potential to get injured.

3. Teacher does not let my mom go to PE.

4. My mom is designated as "classroom keeper" because the teacher was worried about her and didn't want her to injure herself in PE.

These assumptions barred my mom from participating in PE, but growing up I've always thought my mom to be a really active person. When I was in elementary school, my mom would spend the weekends working at a vitamin store in a Korean grocery market. In middle school, she opened her own ice cream store and was there working all day, every day. Then when I was in high school, she had her own coffee shop and didn't hire any employees since it was small enough to be run by one person. Anyone who has run their own business or worked in the food industry knows they require a lot of physical activities, like endlessly shopping at Costco for supplies, lifting things, and standing all day. It is hard work, but my mom accomplished all of this, proving that the assumptions she faced about her abilities growing up were false.

How might things have been different if people hadn't told my mom what she was able to do or not do, and instead let her experiment and try things to see for herself what her abilities were? What my mom wants to emphasize from her experiences is that others should focus on the abilities people do have, rather than the ones they don't.

Now, I'm not saying assumptions are necessarily bad. Assumptions happen because they are assumptions (a.k.a. predictions) we use to research and test things; however, the times when assumptions ARE bad is when they produce bad design or negative experiences that don't align with the user's true needs.

HOW TO BE EFFECTIVE WITH YOUR ASSUMPTIONS
We now know that having assumptions directly affects the final product. We're also human and having assumptions is going to be part of the way we think.

To combat this, here are three things you can do:

1. **Lay it out on the table**. Identify as many assumptions as you possibly can about all the stakeholders you might be affecting. If it is for an elderly population, what

assumptions do you have about the environment they are using your product in? How will this product affect their caretakers or their family?

2. **Have a conversation about assumptions with your team.** Opening a judgment-free conversation zone about assumptions that you and your team members have will benefit everyone. This gives your team the opportunity to share things they may be uncomfortable confronting, and you may be able to uncover other assumptions you didn't realize you had.

3. **Make sure you are including the community you are creating for in the design process.** This message has come up already and will continue to come up, because designing with the user is that important. Testing your products with diverse communities will also expose assumptions.

There are a lot of ways to expose assumptions. What are some ways you have exposed your own?

Identifying assumptions we have can be an awkward, and sometimes even shameful process, but the fact that we are going through it means we are turning toward developing a more inclusive mind. I know we all have embarrassing stories about assumptions (after all, assumptions make an ass out of U and Me [assume=ass+u+me...get it?], an adage my mentor Sonya Cunningham said once, which has stuck with me over the past three years). However, the humbling experiences of exposing these toxic thoughts will lead to developing something bigger than our humility: an inclusive mindset.

LET'S INCLUSIFY

- Practice realizing what assumptions you have of other people and how they could be damaging to the way you think of them.

- Understand that not all assumptions are necessarily bad, since they are like predictions, or hypotheses about things we test. They become bad if we act on them without facts to support them.

- Practice working through your assumptions when creating by: (1) laying them out on the table, (2) talking with your team about them, and (3) including the community you are designing for.

WHAT DO YOU
MEAN, NORMAL?

——

"Normal is an ideal. But it's not reality. Reality is brutal, it's beautiful, it's every shade between black and white, and it's magical."

—TARA KELLY[53]

53   Tara Kelly. *Harmonic Feedback* (Henry Holt and Co., 2010).

I had been playing around with what "normal" meant in my head since middle school, when I had to make a two-minute presentation on it. After the two minutes were up, I didn't remember anything I had said but felt good that I was done with this stressful ordeal and had remembered to maintain good eye contact during it. For the next nine years, I tossed it out of my brain box because the philosophical nature of it exasperated me; however, this concept resurfaced in my junior year of college.

On a bus ride to Golden Gardens Beach with a few fellow Unite UW club members, my emotions rose at what I was hearing from a club member alumna. Unite UW is a club that makes space for domestic, out-of-state, and international students to mingle and become friends, because it was observed that people generally made friends in their respective groups. Students could only be participants for a quarter; however, all alumni are invited to their annual end-of-year party.

This alumna was recounting her recent trip to Japan, complaining about her lack of personal space in that country. She hated how people would reach out and touch her pale hair without asking. She then continued to complain about Asian culture as a whole, and their lack of respect for personal space. "But I know it's just because they're ignorant," she concluded.

Anger boiled as I mentally scoffed. Disregarding her massive generalization, how could she, the foreigner, just show up in a different country and claim that their cultural norms were "ignorant?" How could she not see that it was she who was ignorant of their culture, and that the way she held up her own views on what a "normal" social culture entailed was so stereotypical of her background?

I didn't say anything because, as always, words and logic escaped me when my emotions surged, leaving me speechless. However, reflecting on this interaction under the lens of the concept of normal shows how toxic the concept of what normal is can be.

Later my friend introduced me to the topic of cultural relativism, which is "the ability to understand a culture on its own terms and not to make judgments using the standards of one's own culture."[54] Cultural relativism calls for a person to not judge other cultures based on their own, because it is their own cultural norms they would be using to measure the other culture against. Since "normal" means so many things in different cultures, where did it come from?

WHERE DID NORMAL COME FROM?

Defining things as normal can be disruptive because it leads people to look down on what falls outside of what is categorized as normal. It is limiting, and can be a means for discrimination. Kat Holmes describes the origins of the concept "normal" in her book *Mismatch*. After reading it, I realized this concept has no solid scientific grounds, yet it has made such an impact on our society to the point where people use it as a means to justify looking down on other cultures.

Holmes explains that Adolphe Quetelet, a mathematician, surveyed hundreds of people's bodily dimensions, and found that these dimensions fit into the bell curve (actually called

---

54 Cultural Anthropology, "Cultural Relativism," lumen. [Accessed June 3, 2020].

the Gaussian distribution).[55] The bell curve is what had been proved by Gauss: "That the probability of an event...could be drawn as a normal curve and that the average, or vertical midline, of that curve gave the closest representation of the true nature of that event." Quetelet went out and published this finding, including that "individual people should be measured against that perfect average" of the bell curves he made.

Later on, an economist Vilfredo Pareto made the 80/20 rule, which is that 20 percent of inputs leads to 80 percent of outputs.[56] Over time, since these two theories have come into existence, they became melded together, contributing to this reality: "The common misconception is that the center of the curve represents an 80 percent majority of the population and 80 percent of the important problems to solve."[56]

In conclusion, these two theories weren't even meant for each other. They have been put together to define the idea of normal for design, implying that the other 20 percent of users were not worth designing for. Looking back even further, in an article titled "The History of Being Normal," Dr. Sarah Chaney explained that "before the nineteenth century... the term 'normal' was not usually associated with human behavior. Normal was a mathematical term, referring to something standing at a right angle." Dr. Chaney concluded that "exploring the history of the contested ways in which normal standards have changed or been measured across

55 Kat Holmes, *Mismatch* (Cambridge, MA: The MIT Press, 2018), 93-96.

56 Kevin Kruse, "The 80/20 Rule And How It Can Change Your Life," *Forbes*, May 7, 2016.

different times, places, and cultures contradicts the view that normality is somehow a natural concept."[57]

In Vivienne Porritt's TEDxNorwichED talk, she asks "Who deems who or what, are classed as normal? Is it the normal people who decide?"[58] During a class about personality psychology, I learned that although some people share common patterns of behavior, everyone still has their own uniqueness. This uniqueness is what is called out as being abnormal and defined as such by those who are unique in different ways. Porritt concludes her talk with, "I want to spark a change in our thinking and our language." I used to think language was irrelevant because it is the motives behind what is said that matters; however, labels people are given affect the way others view them, making the controlling factor people act on not the motives but the labels.

HOW NORMAL AFFECTS PERCEPTION

Societally determined definitions of normal have permeated our language, making it discriminatory and degrading to those who are not in that range. The discrimination comes from the way that language makes others feel about the person being described.

A study on teachers proves the consequence of labels. The abstract of the paper "Teacher Expectancies and the Label 'Learning Disabilities'" demonstrates this phenomenon.

---

57 Sara Chaney, "The History of Being Normal," *Being Human*, November 22, 2016.

58 *TEDx Talks*, "A world where normal doesn't exist- celebrating uniqueness." | Vivienne Porritt | TEDxNorwichED," July 16, 2018, video, 9:46.

"Prior to viewing the tape, the control group was told that the child was normal while the experimental group was told that the child was learning disabled...The experimental group rated the child more negatively than did the control group. It was concluded that the label "learning disabled" generates negative expectancies in teachers, which affects their objective observations of behavior and may be detrimental to the child's academic progress."[59]

In this experiment, the child's actions weren't what was making the teachers think they were normal or had a disability, it was what other people told them. This highlights how important it is to be aware of the language we use. After this language came the confirmation bias, making teachers believe whether a child was "normal" or not.

This relates to inclusive design because who we perceive as a normal user group is the core of what makes our creations exclusive. As a society, we need to stop using these labels. The concept of normal was founded by the correlation between two theories that weren't meant for each other and then compounded by confirmation bias.

To prevent being affected by what society generalizes about people, we can implement more inclusive language. By speaking inclusively, as in not defining people by their deviance from societal generalizations, but instead by their actions and abilities, we can move away from labeling those who are

---

59   Glen G. Foster, Carl R. Schmidt, and David Sabatino, "Teacher Expectancies and the Label 'Learning Disabilities,'" *Journal of Learning Disabilities* (1976).

different from us not as "other" but as just different, since we all have differences.

We can also think more inclusively by identifying the fact that our typical life norms have been built by our personal life experiences. These experiences are not always going to be universal, just like the social norms surrounding personal space in Western cultures and in Asia.

LET'S INCLUSIFY

- Practice recognizing why you think of other people or their actions as abnormal—what life experiences made you think and do things the way you do? Was this experience universal?

- Practice examining more carefully who the users of your product will be.

- Practice speaking and thinking more inclusively, being aware that your views will also affect what other people experience.

EMPATHY: A TREND?
LET'S NOT.

"Empathy has some unfortunate features—it is parochial, narrow-minded, and innumerate. We're often at our best when we're smart enough not to rely on it."

—PAUL BLOOM, THE NEW YORKER [60]

---

60   Paul Bloom, "The Baby in the Well," *The New Yorker, May 13, 2013.*

In high school I saw the empathy video about the fox in a hole, the bear who climbs down to be with the fox, and the antelope that silver lines the issues the fox is having.[61] This made me think, "Wow, empathy is really great." I thought it was about sharing emotions with someone facing hardships and understanding them. I put empathy on a golden pedestal of what I should strive to have. However, since then, the concept of empathy has exploded in the design world. Everyone's UX portfolios has the word "empathy" on it (even mine). Company's job descriptions talk about needing empathy. With this hyper focus on empathy, are we actually doing it right? Or do we even know what it is?

A paper about video games and empathy called "Designing Games to Foster Empathy" goes in depth explaining the different forms of empathy. Jonathan Belman from New York University and Mary Flanagan from Dartmouth College identified two types of empathy: cognitive and emotional.[62]

Cognitive empathy → when we intentionally take someone else's point of view.

Emotional empathy →

1. **Parallel**. Where we seek to feel the vicarious experience of another person's emotional state. An example of this would be one person talking about their experiences being blind and then another person putting on a blindfold to

---

61   *The RSA*, "Brené Brown on Empathy," December 10, 2013, video, 2:53.

62   Jonathan Belman, and Mary Flanagan, "Designing Games to Foster Empathy," *Cognitive Technology* 14, No. 2: 5-15.

try and experience the same feeling of being blind. However, this exercise in gaining empathy will not be truly representative of a person's lived experience because of the escapable nature of the experience and the situation in which the person is pretending to be visually impaired.

2. **Reactive**. When we have an emotional response to seeing something happen to someone else. This is like when we watch videos that make us feel strongly for the people in the video (usually followed by a request for donations).

Cognitive empathy, intentionally taking someone else's point of view, has its downfalls for reasons similar to parallel emotional empathy. We won't be able to fully experience something in the same way as the actual users. I tried this myself in middle school, when I decided I would be an atheist for a day to see what it would be like to not believe in God. But, as I soon realized, it doesn't work like that.

There are issues with both types of emotional empathy being relied on in design. With parallel empathy, just replicating an experience to "get into the shoes" of a user isn't going to fully inform that experience and will lead to our own assumptions informing the design based off of the temporary adoption of that experience.

YOU-CENTERED

In my User Centered Design class, a group of students were designing something for runners. To learn about runners, they joined the UW running team. These students were critiqued heavily during their final presentation by guest professionals who were invited to our class. To be honest, my group would have done the same if the members of our user group weren't mental health professionals, whose experience we couldn't participate in due to the private nature of their work. The group who designed for runners were critiqued on how their experience as people who don't identify as runners affected not only their experience of running, but also the runners themselves, when they ran with the UW running club. This critique was based on how, by trying to simulate being a runner, their assumptions of what running is like affected their perception of runners.

Simulating the experience of users also extends to disability, where someone will pretend to have a disability to see what it is like to do things as somebody with that disability.

Arielle Silverman, in her paper about "The Perils of Playing Blind," talks about the unintended consequences of simulating blindness. These consequences include reinforcing misconceptions about people who are blind and their capabilities because of the temporary and escapable nature of simulations. Being blindfolded and going out to do things might simulate the experience of someone who has just lost their sight, but it does not simulate other experiences.[63]

"While the onset of blindness can indeed be traumatic, it is very different from the reality of living with blindness after many years. People adapt to new disabilities over time by mastering alternative techniques, building support networks, and focusing

---

63   Arielle Michal Silverman, "The Perils of Playing Blind: Problems with Blindness Simulation and a Better Way to Teach about Blindness," *Journal of Blindness Innovation and Research* 5, No. 2 (2015).

their attention on areas of their lives that are unaffected by the disability....Furthermore, people who are congenitally disabled never experience the trauma of disability onset at all. Correspondingly, the simulation may barely have any connection to their experience. Simulations cannot capture these nuances and long-term effects. Consequently, simulations can give the mistaken impression that the entirety of being disabled is marked by loss, frustration, and incompetence." [66]

If somebody is trying to experience what it is like to be blind to empathize with someone who is actually blind for a design project, the assumptions they gather from the simulation won't be accurately representative of a blind person's experience (making it you-centered as opposed to user-centered). Additionally, it would be compared to their own experiences of how things work for them.

An example Dr. Silverman uses to explain the negative consequences of assumptions is a preschool aid who simulated being a wheelchair user to experience what it was like for the student she was with. After that simulation, she started helping the student with things that he already showed he could do by himself. The assumptions this aid had after simulating being in a wheelchair led to her giving unsolicited help, which "can prevent children from developing skills and confidence, and it can also harm self-esteem." [66]

At the end of the paper, Dr. Silverman listed some ways that people can simulate disability with more representative outcomes in terms of their experience. Positive activities included skill mastery, where a person would simulate a disability and learn a skill with it, and another was involving the person with the same disability they are trying to simulate in the simulation. This way, the person simulating could learn how the person with a disability does things.

There is something different about how the person gains experience and insight into a person's experience in the last simulation. Instead of a person trying to adopt an experience with the focus on themselves having empathy, it is about the person sharing an experience with the person for whom they are trying to have empathy.

Cynthia Bennet explores this sharing of experiencing as a means of gaining empathy for a user group in her paper, "The Promise of Empathy." Bennet explains different ways to share experience, such as instead of trying to go out and understand someone else's experience, reaching out to form a partnership with them.[64] This shared creation makes way for incorporating more of the user's experience into the design process, as opposed to the designer's understanding of their experience. Additionally, this would avoid mainly incorporating what the designer's experience was in their journey to try and gain empathy for the user.

UNDERSTANDING EXPERIENCES TO STRENGTHEN EMPATHY

Remember Dr. Bricker's story, from "Sexism...It's Everywhere?" In addition to altering the way she taught classes, Dr. Bricker started getting involved with diversity through her work as

---

64   Cynthia L. Bennett, and Daniela K. Rosner, "The Promise of Empathy: Design, Disability, and Knowing the 'Other,'" CHI Conference on Human Factors in Computing Systems Proceedings (2019).

a professor and being on the diversity committee. Although believing she did not know enough to be involved in the diversity meeting, she still participated and empathized with the students for whom she advocated.

One time, when Dr. Bricker was taking a picture of her laser cutter, she took down her Star of David, which was hanging on the wall next to the laser cutter before taking the picture. She became aware about what people would think about this part of her life that she chose to keep private.

"So I took this picture because I wanted to post this [laser cutter]. But usually right there [Dr. Bricker pointed in the picture at an empty part of the wall] is a star. I took it down....I've never been worried about that before. But the interesting thing is there was sort of an eye-opening moment or, I don't know, kind of a transition where I'm realizing, '*Yeah, those are uncomfortable things, but those are what some people have to deal with on a daily basis because of the color of their skin.*'"

Acknowledging her ability to hide this part of her identity hit her strongly. What she took away from this experience is an understanding of what it might feel like to be a minority, and it gave her perspective into what it might feel like to look differently than the majority of society as she, in this moment, felt like a minority in the beliefs of society. This understanding from the experience of wondering what society would think if they learned she was Jewish strengthened her empathy.

It is important to note that this understanding is just a small piece of the experience someone might feel all the time, and that this gives us a taste of something bigger, but not the whole thing.

Feeling like an imposter and trying to advocate for and improve equality for a population we are not part of can seem like we are not doing enough or doing things right. However, I believe we need advocates and makers of inclusion within all types of excluded populations to help open the doors for their voices in the common areas. Additionally, a way to build your personal sense of empathy for marginalized communities can come from being excluded in different parts of life. Although it is not the same, understanding what we are feeling in that moment may be felt exponentially by others is something that will stick with us and motivate us when we feel like an imposter.

What makes me realize and believe in the importance of being inclusive stems from the number of times I find myself standing on the outside of circles. Sometimes socially, with not getting references about SpongeBob or meme. Even now I have no idea how a meme becomes popular and then suddenly it seems like everybody except me knows about it. By the time I discovered the baby Yoda meme, it was "so last week." I've also experienced it physically. In social situations, I try to be engaging and participate, but in the last few years I realize that somehow, even if I started out standing in the circle, I often find myself staring at the backs of the people I was standing in between.

At first, I didn't know this was happening, but once I identified it, I realized how often it happened. Now I get so nervous about being with large groups of people with the expectation to socialize that I try to avoid going out with groups bigger than five or six people. This made going to a club reunion really stressful, to the point where I stood in the bathroom and cried once getting to the building. I hadn't even gone into the room where the reunion was yet because I was worried about what social awkwardness I would face. This same anxiety sometimes kept me in my dorm when my classmates were going out clubbing while studying abroad. The understanding I gain based on these experiences is the emotions of frustration and loneliness that come from being barred from an experience, and the lasting affect it can have.

But what would happen if all I relied on was my understanding of experiences to tell me how things must be for someone else? There are so many differing experiences out there; we cannot expect to have an understanding to relate to all of them. If all we cared about was experiences we could relate to and acknowledge, then what about the ones that we couldn't? This is where empathy fails us.[63]

We cannot rely on empathy to inform us of other people's experiences all the time. We have to acknowledge that we will not always be able to get a sense of how someone else feels about something. We have to acknowledge that since our own emotions are fueled by psychology, which can be tricked into perceiving something as more important than something else based on our relationship to that thing, we cannot rely on our sense of empathy to inform us about whatever that thing is. This is something that we witnessed with the Black Lives Matter movement.

How can someone who has grown up in a primarily white community have any idea what it is like to be scared of police-men, or to know that the judicial system won't be there to support and protect them? How can someone who has the privilege to never have felt loss due to police brutality even have any understanding of the fear and the anger and the frustration fueling the protests? But just because we cannot know or understand does not mean we should not stand up.

If we have understandings from personal experiences, we need to consider thoroughly the implications of what we learned from them, and how to apply them to realizing pieces of experience others might have. If we don't have them, that's okay too—we must realize that we won't know what something might be like and educate ourselves in different ways in how to be an effective ally. Empathy is not something meant to be emotionally moving and used to tell us what causes are important and what causes aren't.[60] Empathy is meant to be something that contributes to our strength as an ally: someone who supports marginalized communities by creating more inclusion.

LET'S INCLSUIFY

- Practice being intentional about building empathy to keep it valuable.

- Be aware of whether you have cognitive or emotional empathy.

- Practice working with, not for, marginalized communities.

PART 4

INCLUSIFY YOUR ACTIONS

This section explores how we can make an impact in inclusive design through our actions. We look at what it means to be an ally and what we can do to build our society inclusively.

"ALLY IS A VERB"

"Many of those who claim to be allies wear the phrase and ideology like an article of clothing. An article that is easily discarded when it's no longer hip or safe to wear."

—GUIDE TO ALLYSHIP[65]

---

65   "Guide to Allyship," Guide to Allyship, accessed on May 25, 2020.

"Where were my allies when I needed them?" she asked as she told me her story.

This question resonated with me. The way she said it, confused and let down, like she expected them to be there, because they said they were there for her but weren't. This pushed me to address the topic of allyship. A topic I didn't want to address at first, because I didn't know anything about it and had only heard of it in a negative light. People talked about how others tried to be allies, but weren't fixing real problems, or weren't there when they needed to be.

Researching this area showed me that what I felt about this space of allyship is common. This feeling of not identifying or acting as an ally from not knowing very much about it, and being scared of doing something wrong, is part of it. Acting on this feeling instead of letting it simmer is what we need to do. We need to put in the time and research to know what it means to be an ally in the field we are passionate about, whether it is the LGBTQ+ community or gender or race. There are advocates in all of these spaces who fight back against the societal oppression that devalues others, and in fighting for what we are passionate about, we will see the lines between communities we are advocating for begin to blur, until we are an advocate for inclusion.

An inclusion advocate in sports, Hudson Taylor, talks about being an ally in his paper "Activating Change Through Allyship."[66] He said that "industry archetypes are the enemy of inclusion," meaning that model stereotypes we imagine when

---

66 Hudson Taylor, "Activating Change Through Allyship," *Journal of Intercollegiate Sport* 8, no. 1 (2015): 37–42.

thinking about a certain industry are adversaries to having an inclusive mindset. When we visualize a type of person who does a specific job, we then categorize all people of that type within that one industry. For example, when I think "accountant," the first image that comes to mind is a young Caucasian man with dark hair wearing a suit, even when I know that when my parents had an accountant, she was an Asian woman.

Taylor explains the implication of this industry archetype in a story about how a well-known, successful female coach was fired from her position. The implication of this was other female coaches not feeling job security despite having a lot of experience and successful accomplishments to show for it. Without allies in the male coach community, this unequal treatment would only persist.

"One reason for this disparate treatment is that women do not have vocal male allies among coaches. The silence of the male coaching community is an implicit endorsement of this biased culture....The lack of opportunities for women as compared with men is without defense [in the coaching industry]. Until those who benefit most from this bias start calling attention to this inequality, the number of women coaching at the highest level may continue to decline."

In this quote, Taylor brings up another point: "those who benefit most from this bias" are the ones with privilege. Privilege is another huge topic, but under the lens of allyship, people with privilege are the ones who should be allies, since they have the means to do it.

BEING WITH

Due to COVID-19 and having remote classes, I decided to drop into a presentation that a PhD graduate was holding about their research with children on the autism spectrum. Kate Ringland did her PhD research through video games. She went into AutCraft, a world created for children with autism within Minecraft, and played. In AutCraft, she was able to interact with the children and observe what they did in the game, making it clear through online forums and in the game that she was a researcher, even wearing a white lab coat so people could identify her as such.

One topic she brought up during our conversation, which is something majorly lacking in the academic research community, is the sense of giving back and maintaining relationships with research participants. Through getting involved with the AutCraft community, sharing what she learns with them, and maintaining relationships, she is able to break out of the typical process of going in, doing the research, and disappearing. When this happens with marginalized communities, there is no tangible give and take—it's just take. To avoid this, people can share their research findings or even build better relationships with their participants.

An example of building better relationships is instead of doing research on people with disabilities, people are starting to change their mindsets so that research is being done with disabled community members. However, even when designing with the users (such as participatory design), nothing typically happens after the prototype is made and the paper is published. There is no direct, tangible benefit from the time people put in to help the research.

A question that Kate is tackling along with a group of other researchers is how to do research that's more equitable.

One thing acting against this is the agenda to publish as many papers as they can. With the main focus being on quantity, "this model hurts people trying to be conscious about equity...making it hard to be an ally and do this kind of research."

Kate's definition of an ally is "being someone who is invested in the care and outcome of a community, do what we need to do to further that community." Kate considers herself an ally in AutCraft because she is "lending legitimacy, giving resources, sharing with them what they need to do without perspective and judgment."

Another thing that makes her more comfortable interacting with this community is how she identifies with being neurodiverse. By sharing some form of common ground, she knows what it is like to be marginalized.

However, even if people don't have a common ground to begin to identify with another person's experience, that doesn't mean they can't still be an ally. In the US 2010 census, it was shown that 76.5 percent of the population identified as "white alone."[70] With such a large majority of the population not identifying with being in a racially marginalized group of people, that would be a lot of people who could be allies. However, even though this lack of common ground with communities may be a deterrent to working at becoming an ally, people still can and need to be allies! In the Guide to Allyship, Amelie Lamont wrote that "allies recognize that though they are not a member of the oppressed group(s) they support, they make a concerted effort to better understand the struggle, every single day. Because an ally might have more privilege (and recognizes said privilege), they are powerful voices *alongside* oppressed ones."[67]

When I asked Kate how people who don't have common ground with the community they want to ally with can become stronger allies, she said that they "need to be open-minded enough, being open to being challenged and wrong about things." She said, "I think it's imperative that other folks become allies." The mindset this requires is "being open, being aware of your own biases, being open to being wrong about things. Once you've practiced that, it's easier to do that with other groups of people."

BEING OPEN

Being open-minded and open to being challenged and wrong about things is a sentiment also shared by influencer Franchesca Ramsey, author of *Well, That Escalated Quickly* and the host of MTV's *Decoded* (highly recommend). When first researching about allyship (and getting tired of reading academic papers about it), the biggest takeaways I had from her video "Five Tips for Being an Ally" were about understanding and using privilege, and that ally is a verb.

Ramsey defines privilege as "some things in life that you don't have to think about that others do." Some things I had

---

67   "United States," QuickFacts, United States Census Bureau, accessed on
      May 25, 2020.

the privilege not to be worried about during the COVID-19 pandemic was, will I have access to internet to complete my assignments? Will I have a place to live? Will I even be able to leave the country to go home to see my family? But from emails by programs I am part of offering support in different ways, and from scrolling through different Facebook groups, I learned that this was definitely not the case for other students.

Understanding the privilege we have comes before our ability to be heard and advocate. Ramsey says to "use your privilege and your voice to educate others but make sure to do it in such a way that does not speak over the community members that you are trying to support or take credit for things they are already saying." This means being there with, not for, and not as. When we mess up, apologize, learn, and keep going.[68]

An example of allyship is the A11Y Rules podcast. Nicolas Steenhout, a web accessibility advocate, created a podcast to inform people about accessibility by focusing on interviewing people with disabilities "about the barriers they encounter on the web."[69] This form of allyship embodies the act of being *with*.

Ramsey's video ends with tip five: "Ally is a Verb." Being an ally is so much more than talking about the disparities; it's acting against them. This action can take the form of speaking when it matters to enact change or acting to support marginalized communities when we see something is not right. [71]

---

68 *Chescaleigh,* "5 Tips for Being An Ally," November 22, 2015, video, 3:31.

69 "About," A11Y Rules, accessed on June 3, 2020.

Being open to listening, being wrong, and learning is one of the most important parts of being an effective ally. With the protests arising from George Floyd's murder, resources about how to be an ally have also been made widely available. We need to not only read but implement what we learn from these resources in order to be an ally to the black community. Furthermore, we need to remember. When protests have died down and the media has moved on, we need to remember how to be an ally, and be an ally for all injustices.

Saying we are there for people makes them think we support them, but when we don't stand up and do it, then it leaves them betrayed and wondering, "Where were my allies when I needed them?" We can avoid this by rising up and developing ourselves as allies, being supporters of our fellow communities to make sure they can be included in the experiences we are included in. Even though the road to being an ally is going to be hard, it is still necessary to make our world more inclusive for everyone.

LET'S INCLUSIFY

- Practice taking actionable steps for allyship.

- Find tangible ways to give back to communities helping your research.

- Be there with, not for—or as—other communities.

BUILDING OUR INCLUSIVE SOCIETY

"We've got a responsibility to live up to the legacy of those who came before us by doing all that we can to help those who come after us."

—MICHELLE OBAMA

Legacy. Who else thinks about *Hamilton* from Lin-Manuel Miranda's musical when they hear the word "legacy"? For a whole year, I listened to the soundtrack again and again. I had listened to the songs on long flights, on the Greyhound back and forth across Washington State, and walking all over campus to classes. This part of the musical always recaptured my attention. I don't know whether it was the way Miranda says it in the soundtrack that makes it jump to mind when I think of legacy.

"Legacy.

What is legacy?

It's planting seeds in a garden you never get to see."

—HAMILTON MUSICAL, LIN-MANUEL MIRANDA[70]

In the musical, Alexander Hamilton describes legacy as something you work for without ever seeing the benefits. This is what it feels like sometimes with inclusive design. We make something inclusive or we find a way to design something inclusively, but then we don't see its immediate impact. We rarely find out how it influences others to be more inclusive within their own projects, but that doesn't mean it isn't making a difference; it will. Whether that impact is making an experience more accessible to a user from a marginalized community or causing another creator to notice and integrate the concept into their work, it will.

---

70 Miranda, Lin-Manuel. "Hamilton: An American Musical." In
    Hamilton: The Revolution. Edited by Jeremy McCarter. New York:
    Grand Central Publishing, 2016.

Everyone I've met making inclusive experiences both locally and in their communities abroad have honored me with their time while writing this book. They've made an immeasurable impact on me and taught me how be more inclusive and how to create more inclusively. They have excited and inspired me to continue my journey building inclusive experiences. This is what we need to do in order to make inclusive design a cultural norm. Through our actions, both big and small we can have an inclusive mindset when approaching work. With this inclusive mindset at work we can create a domino effect and influence others to also think more inclusively. This influence can scale. It can make an impact.

Throughout my journey in learning about inclusive design, I kept asking myself about which was the best way to make an impact on inclusive design. Is it from a top-down approach, where the authority figures assign inclusive guidelines to make the work of makers more inclusive? Or is it from a bottom-up approach where change is implemented by the makers themselves? After some thoughtful deliberation, I settled on the bottom-up approach.

However, in a conversation with Sheri Byrne-Haber, the Head of Accessibility at VMware and previous leader of accessibility at Albertsons and McDonald's, it was brought to my attention that the top-down approach could also have a big impact on the future of inclusivity. This is due to the increasing demand from consumers, particularly the millennial consumers. Millennials have demonstrated they are a group that cares a lot about the values a company represents in addition to the services they provide. In response to this, many companies are partnering only with organizations that represent similar values of inclusivity.

In my discussion with Sheri, she explained the need to induce pressure to become more inclusive from both the top-down and bottom-up approach. She explained, "The mental imagery I usually use when describing this is the garbage pit that Leia, Han and Luke were all trapped in; when you are squeezing from all sides, there is nowhere to go." In the same sense, when people are pushing for inclusion on all sides, the hopeful result would be influencing the middle to design inclusively, which would build our inclusive society. We need both sides to be effective.

The scalability of our inclusive mindsets can be expedited by incorporating inclusion into practice. The current practice of "retrofitting"—going back and fixing exclusive mistakes—isn't a good solution, especially if the same mistakes need to be fixed afterwards. Understanding and creating for inclusion will be crucial in the future of making, and by being inclusive ourselves. We can influence others to understand how they can also be inclusive. Right now, we are seeing more jobs on the market for accessibility, demonstrating that many companies see the need for accessible platforms. Claudio Luis Vera is a nearly thirty-year veteran of user experience design who is now active as an accessibility leader. He envisions that the next decade will reveal more positions within accessibility with the societal realization that there is a large need in this space.

"Entirely new specialized niches will emerge in the accessibility field. They'll be mashups of existing disciplines that will come about from the more complex and intersectional needs of this coming decade."[71]

71   Claudio Luis Vera, "What the 2020s may bring us in accessibility," *Medium*, January 1, 2020.

Where are you going to be when this happens? What are some ways you can prepare for it now? Let these questions guide you:

- **What injustices have been nagging at your mind?** Take out your phone, learn what is contributing to the injustice, what people have been doing to fight it, and contribute to ending it.

- **What's stopping you from doing something?** Everyone has skills. Use yours to make an impact.

- **What are some assumptions your work is based on?** Expose them. Figure out how they happened, and what you can do to end that cycle.

- **How can you make your own community more inclusive?** Share this book with your friends so they can also work to develop a more inclusive mindset.

The biggest problem contributing to our exclusive society is our lack of inclusive practice. Movement toward a more inclusive society has already begun—some of the companies you use every day are already working on being more active in the inclusive space. You can help too. **Practice** developing your inclusive mindset with the exercises covered in this book, **share** your ideas on what inclusivity means to you with your friends and family, but most importantly, **appreciate** the groups which you've been included in.

Together, we can inclusify the world!

ACKNOWLEDGMENTS

I am honored and overwhelmed by the immense support people had for my journey. Without every person—who contributed their time, donations, and motivation—publishing this book would not have been possible.

Thank you to the people whose experiences taught me all I know about creating inclusively, and showed me how essential inclusive design on all levels of making is:

Aaron	Kate Edwards
Allie Thu	Kathryn Ringland
Annika Wildenradt	Lauren Bricker
Bhargavi Rao	Lynsay Whelan
Danielle Obsert Salisbury	Samuel Rajkumar
Jessica Zistatsis	

Thank you to my incredible illustrator, Annie Hanson, who created the beautiful illustrations that introduced many chapters.

Thank you to Michael Blume, Alexander Novokhodko, David Rodney, and Autumn Spriggle, who closely revised my content, adding value and keeping me true to my voice.

Thank you to everyone who contributed to my journey and made publishing this book a reality:

Melissa Birchfield

Steven Himes

Kaye Thornbrugh

David Rodney

Eric Koester

Tristan Donyes

Xitlalit Sanchez

Andrew Davidson

Kyla Wright

Adriana McKinney

Deborah Havens

Susan Rodney

Danielle Oberst Salisbury

Allie Thu

Hannah Kurita

Sheldon Levias

Thea Diep Ton

Zakiya Hanafi

Sonya Cunningham

Theresa Britschgi

Autumn Spriggle

Julie Tolmie

Ulisses Ramales

Caitlin Kidd

Griffen Schwiesow

Saiph Savage

Lyle Lasala

Louisa Sukanta

Kendra Liljenquist

Jessica Schultz

Melody Xu

Jelena Vandenburgh

Marnie Spriggle

Verlanie Rodillas

Harim Sanchez

Arelis Flores

Mara Kage

Jessica Zistatsis

Grace Kariuki

Victoria Mount

Howard Sun

Catherine Newton

Lincoln Pothan

Monserrat Medel

Marie Arnold

Esther Lin

David Blacketer

Agustin Cuevas

Jordan Kussmann

Leah Tran

Tewolde Tekle

Christine Everdell

Annie Hanson

Kelsey Gabel

Ross Hunnicutt

Jaewon Choi

Jessica Birchfield

Ivan Montero

Alexander Munch · Alexander Novokhodko
Daniel Le Compte · Lauren Bricker
Loni Shugars · Aaron Joya
Hunter Stratton · Srinithi Latha
Irini Spyridakis · Sheri Byrne-Haber
Raine Reynolds · Claudio Luis Vera
Abraham Mendoza · Grady Thompson
Muge Karagoz · Dean Hamack
Melanie Rodney · Omar Bonilla
Indpreet Kaur · Inhyang Lim
Don Humphrey · Michael Blume
Martha Bedford

An enormous thanks to Eric Koester, who guided me on this journey of writing; Brian Bies, who lead me through the publishing process; and Nick Manusco, Alaisha Verdeflor, and Ryan Porter, my editors whose thoughts and feedback helped me become confident in my message, and everyone else at New Degree Press who helped create this book.

Thank you to all the new connections I met on LinkedIn, who responded to my random messages, expressed how meaningful it is to pursue inclusive design, and welcomed me into your community.

And lastly, thank you to anyone else who might have not been listed. Without everyone's support, I could not have accomplished this. Thank you.

APPENDIX

INTRODUCTION

"Inclusion and Employee Diversity: Here are the Numbers." Analytics in HR. https://www.analyticsinhr.com/blog/inclusion-employee-diversity-numbers/.

Teamable. "Six Statistics That Will Convince You to Prioritize Diversity & Inclusion." Teamable Blog. https://blog.teamable.com/6-statistics-that-will-convince-you-to-prioritize-diversity-inclusion.

United Nations. "The Universal Declaration of Human Rights." Universal Declaration of Human Rights. https://www.un.org/en/universal-declaration-human-rights/index.html.

World Health Organization. "Disability and Health." Newsroom. https://www.who.int/news-room/fact-sheets/detail/disability-and-health.

THE TL;DR HISTORY OF INCLUSIVE DESIGN

Begos, Kevin. "The American eugenics movement after World War II." *INDY Week.* May 18, 2011. https://indyweek.com/news/american-eugenics-movement-world-war-ii-part-1-3/.

Connell, Bettye Rose, Mike Jones, Ron Mace, Jim Mueller, Abir Mullick, Elaine Ostroff, Jon Sanford, Ed Steinfeld, Molly Story, and Gregg Vanderheiden. "The Principles of Universal Design." April 1, 1997. https://projects.ncsu.edu/ncsu/design/cud/about_ud/udprinciplestext.htm?fbclid=IwAR1761UflQV9aF-xfilm5ILVbgj-lIEXDF2uOWS6-mgx5MTnYNYcpfImtcw.

Institute for Human Centered Design. "History." Inclusive Design. https://www.humancentereddesign.org/inclusive-design/history.

Jim Thatcher, Paul Bohman, Michael Burks, Cynthia Waddell, Bob Regan, Shawn Lawton Henry, and Mark Urban. *Constructing Accessible Websites* (Apress, 2002).

Lambert, Steven. "Designing for Accessibility and Inclusion." *Smashing Magazine,* April 9, 2018. https://www.smashingmagazine.com/2018/04/designing-accessibility-inclusion/.

I HAD NO ONE TO HUG

Bichell, Rae Ellen. "Scientists Start to Tease Out the Subtler Ways Racism Hurts Health." *NPR*, November 11, 2017.
https://www.npr.org/sections/health-shots/2017/11/11/562623815/scientists-start-to-tease-out-the-subtler-ways-racism-hurts-health.

"Data Leak Reveals How China 'Brainwashes' Uighurs in Prison Camps." *BBC*. November 24, 2019.
https://www.bbc.com/news/world-asia-china-50511063.

Institute of Educational Science. "Characteristics of Public School Teachers," National Center for Education Statistics.
https://nces.ed.gov/programs/coe/indicator_clr.asp.

Nefas, Li. "Gamers Are Getting Upset over 'Forced Diversity', but This 'Straight White Dude' Shuts Them down in a Viral Twitter Thread." *Bored Panda*. 2019.
https://www.boredpanda.com/gaming-forced-diversity/?utm_source=google&utm_medium=organic&utm_campaign=organic.

SEXISM...IT'S EVERYWHERE

Blow, Charles M. "Checking My Male Privilege." *New York Times*, October 29, 2017.
https://www.nytimes.com/2017/10/29/opinion/checking-my-male-privilege.html.

Bradford, Laurence. "15 of the Most Powerful Women in Tech." *The Balance Careers*. June 25, 2019.
https://www.thebalancecareers.com/powerful-women-in-tech-2071172.

Cunningham, Bridget. "Mildred Dresselhaus, a Driving Force for Women in STEM." *COMSOL Blog*. March 7, 2016.
https://www.comsol.com/blogs/mildred-dresselhaus-a-driving-force-for-women-in-stem/.

"Institute Professor Emerita Mildred Dresselhaus, a pioneer in the electronic properties of materials, dies at 86" *MIT News*. February 21, 2017.
http://news.mit.edu/2017/institute-professor-emerita-mildred-dresselhaus-dies-86-0221.

MAKERS. "She Invented the Tiny Tech That Allows You to Watch Videos on Your Phone." October 30, 2018. Video, 1:30.
https://www.youtube.com/watch?v=nHf5bonkEKo.

"The Latest Stats on Women in Tech." The Muse.
https://www.themuse.com/advice/the-latest-stats-on-women-in-tech.

Zheng, Wei, Ronit Kark, and Alyson Meister. "How Women Manage the Gendered Norms of Leadership." *Harvard Business Review*. November 28, 2018.
https://hbr.org/2018/11/how-women-manage-the-gendered-norms-of-leadership.

THE COMPLEXITIES OF ACCESSIBILITY

Centers for Disease Control and Prevention. "CDC: 1 in 4 US Adults Live with a Disability." CDC Newsroom.
https://www.cdc.gov/media/releases/2018/p0816-disability.html

Sydik, Jeremy. *Designing Accessible Web Sites: 36 Keys to Creating Content for Al Audience and Platforms.* Pragmatic Bookshelf, 2007.

Thatcher, Jim, Paul Bohman, Michael Burks, Cynthia Waddell, Bob Regan, Shawn Lawton Henry, and Mark Urban. *Constructing Accessible Websites* (Apress, 2002)

United Nations. "The Universal Declaration of Human Rights." Universal Declaration of Human Rights. https://www.un.org/en/universal-declaration-human-rights/.

"Why Forrest Stump?" Forrest Stump. Accessed on June 4, 2020. http://www.forreststump.org.

AGEISM, A BACKWARDS PHENOMENON

Applewhite, Ashton. *This Chair Rocks: A Manifesto Against Ageism.* Networked Books, 2016.

Asay, Matt. "Jimmy Wales to Silicon Valley: Grow up and Get over Your Age Bias." *readwrite.* September 27, 2013. https://readwrite.com/2013/09/27/jimmy-wales-to-silicon-valley-grow-up/#awesm=~ojeuVFGfNSkpnn.

Kita, Joe. "Workplace Age Discrimination Still Flourishes in America." *AARP.* December 30, 2019. https://www.aarp.org/work/working-at-50-plus/info-2019/age-discrimination-in-america.html.

Sandra L. Colby and Jennifer M Ortman. "Projections of the Size and Composition of the US Population: 2014 to 2060." *United States Census Bureau.* March 2015. https://www.census.gov/content/dam/Census/library/publications/2015/demo/p25-1143.pdf.

World Health Organization. "Ageism." Ageing and life-course. https://www.who.int/ageing/ageism/en/.

A COMPARISON BETWEEN DESIGN AND POLITICS

"Best 100 Companies for Women's Leadership Development." *Diversity Woman.* https://www.diversitywoman.com/best-100-companies-for-womens-leadership-development/.

Poodry, Clifton A. "Diversity: Why Is It Important and How Can It Be Achieved?" *National Institute of General Medical Sciences,* 2003. https://www.ncbi.nlm.nih.gov/books/NBK36307/.

Rener, Sylvester. "Diversity in Leadership and Its Impact on Society as a Whole." *Women 2.* May 30 2019. https://women2.com/2019/05/30/diversity-in-leadership-and-its-impact-on-society-as-a-whole/.

LET'S TALK BUSINESS

"Designing for Screen Reader Compatibility." *WebAIM.* https://webaim.org/techniques/screenreader/.

"The WebAIM Million." *WebAIM.*
https://webaim.org/projects/million/.

Clark, Joe. *Building Accessible Websites.* New Riders Press, 2002.

Thatcher, Jim, Paul Bohman, Michael Burks, Cynthia Waddell, Bob Regan, Shawn Lawton Henry, and Mark Urban. *Constructing Accessible Websites.* Apress, 2002.

Williams, Greg. "The Huge Cost of Ignoring Accessibility When Designing Your Website." *The Next Web.* September 27, 2019.
https://thenextweb.com/podium/2019/09/27/the-huge-cost-of-ignoring-accessibility-when-designing-your-website/.

INCLUDING CULTURES

Associated Press. "Saudi Flags on Burger Bags: A Big MacStake : Marketing: Muslims Complained That McDonald's World Cup Packaging Sent Koran Verse to the Trash Bin ." *Los Angeles Times.* June 8, 1994.
https://www.latimes.com/archives/la-xpm-1994-06-08-fi-1752-story.html.

Beveridge, Dirk. "McDonald's Backs off Promotion That Offended Muslims; Coca-Cola Draws Fire ." *AP News.* June 8, 1994.
https://apnews.com/dddca737b73fdf7316653cbf54e8c1d3.

Edwards, Kate. "Indigenous Issues." *MultiLingual.* September, 2014.

Lynn, K.T. "Design Matters: Engineering Design is Facing an Unconscious Bias Problem." *The Warren Centre.* May 17, 2019.
https://thewarrencentre.org.au/design-matters-engineering-design-unconscious-bias-problem/.

Wijman, Tom. "The Global Games Market Will Generate $152.1 Billion in 2019 as the US Overtakes China as the Biggest Market." *New Zoo.* June 18, 2019.
https://newzoo.com/insights/articles/the-global-games-market-will-generate-152-1-billion-in-2019-as-the-u-s-overtakes-china-as-the-biggest-market/.

INNOVATING FOR INCLUSION

Bailey, Erika. "Beyond Buzzword: Innovation and Design Thinking." *Medium.* August 20, 2019.
https://medium.com/the-moment-is/beyond-buzzword-innovation-and-design-thinking-44c11dfd4fd9.

Lorman, Claire. "Practicing What We Preach on Inclusivity." *Medium.* December 16, 2018.
https://medium.com/frog-voices/practicing-what-we-preach-on-inclusivity-35284aa00d10.

Merriam-Webster. s.v. "Definition of innovation."
https://www.merriam-webster.com/dictionary/innovation.

Objectified, directed by Gary Hustwit (2009; Plexi Productions), Documentary.

Sadlier, Heath. "Tackling Assumption Monsters by Embracing Ambiguity and Curiosity." *Medium.* May 27, 2017.
https://medium.com/@heathsplosion/tackling-assumption-monsters-by-embracing-ambiguity-and-curiosity-b1831e2dd51d.

Teamable. "Six Statistics That Will Convince You to Prioritize Diversity & Inclusion."
Teamable Blog.
https://blog.teamable.com/6-statistics-that-will-convince-you-to-prioritize-
diversity-inclusion.

INTERSECTIONALITIES OF INCLUSION
Baca, Marie C. "Why Emoji Are—Finally—Becoming More Diverse." *The
Washington Post.* July 17, 2019.
https://www.washingtonpost.com/technology/2019/07/18/why-emoji-are-finally-
becoming-more-diverse/.

Burge, Jeremy. "Facebook Reveals Most and Least Used Emojis." *Emojipedia. July 13, 2018.*
https://blog.emojipedia.org/facebook-reveals-most-and-least-used-emojis/.

Cohn, Neil. "Will Emoji Become a New Language?" *BBC Future.* October 13, 2015.
https://www.bbc.com/future/article/20151012-will-emoji-become-a-new-language.

Kho, Halle. "Taking Risks Inside the Design Process." *frog* (blog).
https://www.frogdesign.com/designmind/taking-risks-design-process.

Shift Labs. "DRIP ASSIST." DripAssist Human.
https://www.shiftlabs.com.

Unicode. "What is Unicode?" General Information.
https://unicode.org/standard/WhatIsUnicode.html.

EFFECTIVE-IZING ASSUMPTIONS
Taylor, Hudson. "Activating Change Through Allyship," *Journal of Intercollegiate
Sport* 8, no. 1 (2015): 37—42.
https://journals.ku.edu/jis/article/view/10087/9517.

WHAT DO YOU MEAN, NORMAL??
Cultural Anthropology, "Cultural Relativism," lumen. [Accessed June 3, 2020].
https://courses.lumenlearning.com/culturalanthropology/chapter/cultural-relativism/.

Foster, Glen G., Carl R. Schmidt, and David Sabatino. "Teacher Expectancies and
the Label 'Learning Disabilities.'" *Journal of Learning Disabilities* (1976).
https://journals.sagepub.com/doi/abs/10.1177/002221947600900209.

Holmes, Kat. *Mismatch.* Cambridge, MA: The MIT Press, 2018.

Kelly, Tara. *Harmonic Feedback.* Henry Holt and Co., 2010.

Kruse, Kevin. "The 80/20 Rule and How It Can Change Your Life." *Forbes.* May 7, 2016.
https://www.forbes.com/sites/kevinkruse/2016/03/07/80-20-rule/#75f957943814.

Sara Chaney. "The History of Being Normal." *Being Human.* November 22, 2016.
https://beinghumanfestival.org/the-history-of-being-normal/.

TEDx Talks. "A World Where Normal Doesn't Exist—Celebrating Uniqueness. |
Vivienne Porritt | Tedxnorwiched." July 16, 2018. Video, 9:46.
https://www.youtube.com/watch?v=YVbtBtw9Tho.

EMPATHY: A TREND? LET'S NOT.

Bloom, Paul. "The Baby in the Well." *The New Yorker*. May 13, 2013.
https://www.newyorker.com/magazine/2013/05/20/the-baby-in-the-well.

Belman, Jonathan and Mary Flanagan. "Designing Games to Foster Empathy,"
Cognitive Technology 14, No. 2: 5-15.
https://tiltfactor.org/wp-content/uploads2/cog-tech-si-g4g-article-1-belman-and-
flanagan-designing-games-to-foster-empathy.pdf.

Bennett, Cynthia L. and Daniela K. Rosner. "The Promise of Empathy: Design,
Disability, and Knowing the 'Other,'" CHI Conference on Human Factors in
Computing Systems Proceedings (2019).
https://doi.org/10.1145/3290605.3300528.

Silverman, Arielle Michal. "The Perils of Playing Blind: Problems with Blindness
Simulation and a Better Way to Teach about Blindness," *Journal of Blindness
Innovation and Research* 5, No. 2 (2015).
https://www.nfb.org/images/nfb/publications/jbir/jbir15/jbir050201.html.

The RSA. "Brené Brown on Empathy." December 10, 2013. Video, 2:53.
https://www.youtube.com/watch?time_
continue=167&v=1Evwgu369Jw&feature=emb_logo.

"ALLY IS A VERB"

A11Y Rules. "About." Accessed on June 3, 2020.
https://a11yrules.com/about/.

Chescaleigh. "5 Tips for Being an Ally." November 22, 2015. Video, 3:31.
https://www.youtube.com/watch?v=_dg86g-QlMo.

Guide to Allyship. "Guide to Allyship." Accessed on May 25, 2020.
https://guidetoallyship.com/#why-allies-are-necessary.

Taylor, Hudson. "Activating Change Through Allyship." *Journal of Intercollegiate
Sport* 8, no. 1 (2015): 37—42.
https://journals.ku.edu/jis/article/view/10087/9517.

United States Census Bureau. "United States." QuickFacts. Accessed on May 26, 2020.
https://www.census.gov/quickfacts/fact/table/US/PST045219.

BUILDING OUR INCLUSIVE SOCIETY

Miranda, Lin-Manuel. "Hamilton: An American Musical." In *Hamilton: The
Revolution*. Edited by Jeremy McCarter. New York: Grand Central Publishing, 2016.

Vera, Claudio Luis. "What the 2020s may bring us in accessibility." *Medium*. January
1st, 2020.
https://medium.com/@claudioluisvera/what-the-2020s-may-bring-us-in-
accessibility-4e9bbc73ab32.

Made in the USA
Columbia, SC
10 August 2020